AIRCRAFT OF THE ACES

132 *JAGDGESCHWADER* 53 'PIK-AS' Bf 109 ACES OF 1940

SERIES EDITOR TONY HOLMES

132

AIRCRAFT OF THE ACES

Chris Goss

JAGDGESCHWADER 53 'PIK-AS' Bf 109 ACES OF 1940

OSPREY PUBLISHING

First published in Great Britain in 2017 by Osprey Publishing
PO Box 883, Oxford, OX1 9PL, UK
1385 Broadway, 5th Floor, New York, NY 10018, USA

E-mail: info@ospreypublishing.com

OSPREY is a trademark of Osprey Publishing, a division of Bloomsbury
Publishing Plc.

Osprey Publishing, part of Bloomsbury Publishing Plc

A CIP catalogue record for this book is available from the British Library

ISBN: 978 1 4728 1871 3
PDF e-book ISBN: 978 1 4728 1872 0
e-Pub ISBN: 978 1 4728 1873 7

Edited by Tony Holmes and Philip Jarrett
Cover Artwork by Mark Postlethwaite
Aircraft Profiles by Chris Davey
Index by Angela Hall
Originated by PDQ Digital Media Solutions, UK
Printed in China through World Print Ltd

17 18 19 20 21   10 9 8 7 6 5 4 3 2 1

Osprey Publishing supports the Woodland Trust, the UK's leading woodland
conservation charity. Between 2014 and 2018 our donations will be spent on
their Centenary Woods project in the UK.

Front Cover
On 12 August 1940, JG 53 was tasked with carrying out a 'Freie Jagd' off Portsmouth and the Isle of Wight in support of Ju 88s of KG 51 that were attacking Portsmouth harbour and Ventnor radar station on the Isle of Wight. Leading 1./JG 53 was Hauptmann Hans-Karl Mayer, who was flying a Bf 109E-4 coded 'White 8'. His *Rottenflieger* was Unteroffizier Heinrich Rühl in a Bf 109E-1 coded 'White 10'. Flying at 8500 m, Mayer spotted three Hurricanes below attacking a lone Bf 110 at 1220 hrs, and although he quickly engaged the enemy fighters the Bf 110 pilot bailed out. Mayer selected the right Hurricane and Rühl the left, the former firing a total of 20 20 mm shells and 80 7.92 mm machine gun rounds into the RAF fighter, which immediately burst into flames and dived into the sea for what would be Mayer's tenth victory of the war. Having already exhausted his supply of cannon shells, Rühl fired 200 machine gun rounds at his Hurricane, which then hit the sea in a gentle curve.

Mayer now turned his attention to the remaining Hurricane, which had been engaged by the rest of his *Staffel*. This combat was not as one-sided, however, for his Bf 109E was hit six times. Mayer's combat report noted;

'After my first kill I flew back to the dogfight with the last remaining Hurricane against several aircraft of my *Staffel*. I immediately attacked and was able to open fire twice, and also received some hits myself. The damaged aircraft tried to escape in the direction of the coast but I stayed close to it, while my *Staffel* lost me in the haze. At first it made only slight evasive actions, and so I was able to get in several well-aimed bursts. The aircraft started emitting black smoke, went down in a shallow dive and disintegrated on impact.'

Mayer had achieved his second victory of the mission, firing ten cannon and 250 machine gun rounds at the Hurricane, which, after hitting the sea, sank immediately.

Although it cannot be said for certain, it is believed that Mayer and Rühl accounted for Plt Off John Harrison, Acting Flt Lt Wilhelm Pankratz and Sgt Josef Kwiecinski of No 145 Sqn, all of whom were reported missing in action off the Isle of Wight at times that matched the three German claims (*Cover artwork by Mark Postlethwaite*)

CONTENTS

INTRODUCTION

On 15 March 1937 *Jagdgeschwader* (JG) 334 was formed. Commanded by former World War 1 ace Oberst Bruno Loerzer, *Stab.*/JG 334, I. *Gruppe*, commanded by Hauptmann Hubert Merhart von Bernegg, and II. *Gruppe*, led by Hauptmann Hans-Detlev Herhudt von Rohden, were initially based at Mannheim-Sandhofen. *Stab* and I./JG 334 soon moved to Wiesbaden-Erbenheim (formerly a trotting racetrack on the southeastern outskirts of Wiesbaden), via Frankfurt Rebstock, in May 1937, however. III./JG 334 was not formed until July of the following year. The *Geschwader* was originally equipped with Arado Ar 68E biplane fighters, but early in 1938 it began converting to the Messerschmitt Bf 109B.

As with most other frontline units within the Luftwaffe at this time, JG 334 sent a number of its pilots to Spain to fly with the *Legion Condor* in the Spanish Civil War, as the tables opposite show. Many of these *Jagdflieger* went on to be successful and highly decorated fighter pilots in World War 2, although few would survive the conflict.

One pilot whose name stands out was Werner Mölders. Born in Gelsenkirchen on 18 March 1913, he joined the German military in 1931 and began training as a pilot in 1934. His first frontline posting was to JG 134, and he became the *Staffelkapitän* of 1./JG 334 upon its formation. He did not arrive in Spain until the middle of April 1938, after which he took command of *Jagdgruppe* 88's 3. *Staffel* from Oberleutnant Adolf Galland – another pilot who would become a successful ace, despite having left Spain

On 15 March 1937 *Jagdgeschwader* (JG) 334 was formed under the command of former World War 1 ace Oberst Bruno Loerzer, who is seen here in the late summer of 1940 with Reichsmarschall Hermann Göring. The two men were good friends, having served together as a highly successful reconnaissance crew on the Western Front. By the time this photograph was taken Loerzer had been promoted to *General der Flieger* and made commander of II. *Fliegerkorps (John Weal)*

JG 334 pilots with victories (confirmed and unconfirmed)

NAME	VICTORIES
Oberleutnant Hubertus von Bonin	1
Leutnant Heinz Bretnütz	2
Unteroffizier Günther Freund	2
Leutnant Rudolf Goy	3
Oberfeldwebel Heinz Grimmling	1
Hauptmann Harro Harder	11
Unteroffizier Willibald Hien	4
Oberfeldwebel Fritz Hillmann	3
Hauptmann Lothar von Janson	1
Unteroffizier Karl Kolb	1
Unteroffizier Erich Kuhlmann	4
Leutnant Wolfgang Lippert	5
Oberleutnant Hans-Karl Mayer	8
Oberleutnant Werner Mölders	14
Oberleutnant Rolf Pingel	6
Oberfeldwebel Ignaz Prestele	4
Unteroffizier Bernhard Seufert	3
Unteroffizier Alfred Stark	1

Other JG 334 pilots known to have flown in Spain

Oberleutnant Ernst Boenig
Oberleutnant Hubert Kroeck
Oberleutnant Alfred von Loijewski
Oberleutnant Günther Schulze-Blanck
Leutnant Werner Ursinus
Oberleutnant Wolf-Dietrich Wilcke

Oberst Loerzer's JG 334 was initially equipped with the Arado Ar 68E biplane fighter, with this particular example from 1. *Staffel* photographed at Frankfurt Rebstock possibly being assigned to future ace Feldewebel Franz Götz (*John Weal*)

without a single victory to his name because he primarily flew ground attack missions in the obsolescent Heinkel He 51. Mölders scored his first and second kills on 15 July 1938, and by the time he handed over his *Staffel* to Oberleutnant Hubertus von Bonin at the start of December 1938 he had shot down 14 aircraft, his last being claimed on 3 November 1938.

I./JG 334's arrival at Wiesbaden-Erbenheim in May 1937 was marked by a ceremonial parade through the town. To the strain of martial music provided by the band in the background, Oberleutnant Werner Mölders leads his 1. *Staffel* past the reviewing stand (*John Weal*)

As the top scorer of the *Legion Condor* he was awarded the Spanish Cross in Gold with Swords and Diamonds, and on his return to Germany he was posted on to the Staff of the *Inspektor der Jagdflieger* of the *Reichsluftfahrtministerium* (RLM) in Berlin. Here, Mölders' extensive combat experience as a fighter pilot was put to good use in developing future tactics and techniques.

Meanwhile, JG 334, now commanded by Oberstleutnant Werner Junck, another World War 1 fighter pilot, had been re-designated JG 133 in November 1938 (and was formed of just I. and II. *Gruppe*). In March 1939 Werner 'Vati' Mölders returned to reassume command of 1./JG 133. His fellow *Staffelkapitäne* were also ex-*Legion Condor* pilots, namely Oberleutnant Rolf Pingel in 2. *Staffel* and Hauptmann Lothar von Janson in 3. *Staffel*. Shortly thereafter von Janson took over command of I. *Gruppe* and was replaced by Oberleutnant Wolfgang Lippert.

Similarly, II./JG 133 was also commanded by a mix of combat veterans and relatively inexperienced pilots. Hauptmann Hubert Merhart von Bernegg had moved from being *Gruppenkommandeur* of I./JG 133 to II. *Gruppe* the previous year. Ex-*Legion Condor* pilot Oberleutnant Hubert Kroeck commanded 4. *Staffel* and fellow Spanish war veteran Oberleutnant Rudolf Goy led 5. *Staffel*, but 6. *Staffel* was headed by Hauptmann Günther *Freiherr* von Maltzahn, who had not flown in Spain. Within five months he replaced von Bernegg as II. *Gruppe Kommandeur*, 6. *Staffel* then being led by Oberleutnant Heinz Bretnütz, who had flown in Spain.

At the start of May 1939 JG 133 was re-designated JG 53. Now equipped with the latest Bf 109E-1s and E-3s, the 'Pik-As' (Ace of Spades) *Geschwader*, as it was soon to be known, was still flying from Wiesbaden-Erbenheim when German troops invaded Poland on 1 September 1939. Two days later France and Great Britain declared war on Germany, and it was not long before I. and II./JG 53 were in combat.

Unteroffizier Kurt Sauer of 9./JG 53 is sat on the wing leading edge of a Bf 109E from his *Staffel* that has just been adorned with the 'Pik-As' badge. Sauer shot down three aircraft in 1940, and his tally stood at nine by the time he was made a PoW on 16 July 1941. The 'Pik-As' emblem was applied to all of JG 53's aircraft following its adoption by the unit's new *Kommodore*, Generalmajor Hans Klein (himself a 22-victory Word War 1 ace), upon him taking over from Oberstleutnant Werner Junck in late October 1939

CHAPTER ONE

TO WAR

Although still based at Wiesbaden-Erbenheim when German troops invaded Poland on 1 September 1939, elements of I./JG 53 dispersed to a meadow away from the airfield as a precautionary measure against possible enemy air attacks (*John Weal*)

I f the 'Pik-As' pilots thought they would immediately be in combat with French aircraft, they were wrong. Despite operating in the Saarbrücken/ Trier area, which was bounded by neutral Luxembourg, Germany and France, it took almost a week before anything happened. When it did, the first casualty was almost Werner Mölders. Some records state that his Bf 109 was damaged in combat with French Curtiss H-75As of *Groupe de Chasse* (GC) II/4 on the morning of 8 September 1939, resulting in him force-landing behind German lines near Birkenfeld. However, although his log book confirms he took off from Wiesbaden at 0930 hrs that day on a flight over the frontline, it does not mention any encounter with enemy aircraft before he force-landed. Apparently his aircraft overturned and he suffered minor injuries that kept him off flying until 15 September.

While Mölders was recuperating, his *Staffel* scored the *Geschwader*'s first victory of the war when former *Legion Condor* pilot Oberfeldwebel Heinz Grimmling shot down a Bloch MB.131 reconnaissance-bomber – which he misidentified as an RAF Blenheim – of *Groupes Aériennes de Reconnaissance* (GAR) 14 at 1136 hrs on 9 September, killing three of its crew and wounding one. Three hours later, Leutnant Wilhelm Hoffmann of 3./JG 53 shot down a Bloch MB.200 bomber, believed to be from *Groupe de Bombardement* (GB) I/31, which crashed near Zweibrücken. Its five crew, including GB I/31's commandant, Lt Col Enselem, were captured.

The following day saw three more victories for 1. *Staffel*, Oberleutnant Rolf Pingel of 2./JG 53 adding one more to his six victories in Spain. These claims were all for ANF Le Mureaux 113 parasol-wing all-metal monoplanes that were being used by *Groupes Aériénnes d'Observation* (GAO) 1/506 to perform reconnaissance missions along the frontline, the *Armée de l'Air* reporting the loss of three that day. Pingel had spotted two of the parasol monoplanes at 4500 ft over the Saarlautern area, diving down on one of them from 6000 ft – he sent his target spiralling away in flames near Ensdorf. The wreck of the ANF Le Mureaux 113 was subsequently inspected by German personnel, its two-man crew having been killed in the crash.

There were further inconclusive clashes with H-75As (of GC II/5) and Morane-Saulnier MS.406s (of GC I/3) on 11 and 15 September, respectively, followed by a more conclusive encounter on the 17th when five Bf 109Es from I./JG 53 downed an MB.131 from *Groupes de Reconnaissance* (GR) I/22 over Morsbach. Its demise was credited to Hauptmann Dr Erich Mix (who had claimed two victories flying fighters with JG 54 in World War 1) and Leutnant Wilfried Balfanz. Both pilots would later achieve ace status.

20 September proved to be a field day for JG 53, with II. *Gruppe* claiming its first victories. At 0955 hrs Oberleutnant Heinz Bretnütz of 6./JG 53 was credited with shooting down a balloon, and two hours later Leutnante Albert Richert and Kurt Liedtke of 5. *Staffel* claimed two 'Blenheim IVs' near Bitsch. This was the first time that JG 53 had met the RAF, and the pilots' aircraft recognition was a bit awry as they actually shot down two Fairey Battles of No 88 Sqn that were engaged on a reconnaissance mission. Flg Off Reginald Graveley, the pilot of one of the aeroplanes, managed to crash-land behind Allied lines. AC1 D J John was killed and Sgt W S Everett sustained extensive burns, while Graveley himself was also badly burned while pulling Everett from the wreckage to a place of safety and then returning to the aircraft to try to recover the body of his gunner. Sadly, Everett succumbed to his wounds several hours later. Reginald Graveley was awarded the OBE later that year for his efforts to save his crew. The crew of the second Battle, flown by Flt Sgt Douglas Page, were killed.

This photograph of 2. *Staffel* pilots was taken in the autumn of 1939. They are, from left to right, Unteroffizier Hans Kornatz (rear – 36 victories, survived), Leutnant Rudolf Schmid (two victories, killed on 15 September 1940), Leutnant Wilhelm Heidemeier (two victories, killed on 11 July 1941), Unteroffizier Franz Kaiser (nine victories, PoW from 21 April 1942), Stabsfeldwebel Ignaz Prestele (20 victories, killed on 4 May 1942), Oberleutnant Rolf Pingel (28 victories, PoW from 10 July 1941), Feldwebel Franz Gawlik (five victories, survived), Unteroffizier Josef Wurmheller (102 victories, killed on 22 June 1944), unknown, Leutnant Walter Rupp (two victories, PoW from 17 October 1940) and Leutnant Walter Radlick (four victories, killed on 2 October 1940)

That afternoon I./JG 53 claimed four victories, with all of them being credited to successful pilots from the Spanish campaign. The *Gruppe*'s first victory on 20 September had in fact come at 0755 hrs when future ace Oberfeldwebel Ignaz 'Igel' Prestele of 2./JG 53 shot down a balloon (the French lost three observation balloons to the Luftwaffe in the area south of Saarbrücken on this date). Three-and-a-half hours later an unidentified MS.406 was claimed by Oberfeldwebel Willibald Hein, although no Morane-Saulnier fighters were in fact lost that day. At 1345 hrs I./JG 53 intercepted an ANF Le Mureaux 115 of GAO 507 on a reconnaissance mission over the Saar valley, the aeroplane being attacked by Spanish war veteran and future ace Oberleutnant Günther Schulze-Blanck (who claimed that he attacked a 'Potez') and Oberfeldwebel Hein. The crew of the observation aircraft managed to force-land their shot up machine just behind the French frontline.

At 1450 hrs it was the turn of Unteroffizier Günther Freund of 1. *Staffel* and his *Staffelkapitän*, Hauptmann Werner Mölders, to claim their first victories of the war when they attacked and shot down two H-75s of GC II/5 between Contz and Sierck. It was reported that six machines from this unit had been covering another reconnaissance aircraft over the Apach-Büdingen sector when three of the fighters acting as high cover were drawn away by a lone Henschel Hs 126 observation aeroplane. The French pilots believed that the latter aircraft had deliberately lured them into a trap. Sgt Pechaud managed to force-land at St Mihiel without injury to himself, but Sgt Quéguiner, believed to be Mölders' victim, bailed out wounded west of Merzig. Mölders' combat report read as follows;

'I took off with my *Schwarm* [section of four aircraft] at 1427 hrs to intercept six enemy monoplanes reported south of Trier. As the *Schwarm* overflew the River Saar near Merzig at 4500 m, six machines were sighted south of Conz (*sic*) at 5000 m. I climbed above the enemy in a wide curve to the north and carried out a surprise attack on the rearmost machine. I opened fire from approximately 50 m, whereupon the Curtiss began to fishtail. After a further lengthy burst, smoke came out of the machine and individual pieces flew off it. It then tipped forward into a dive and I lost sight of it, as I had to defend myself against other opponents newly arriving on the scene.'

Mölders' success was confirmed by his three *Schwarm* members, who further reported that the French pilot bailed out before the H-75A crashed in flames to the west of Merzig. In return, 3./JG 53 had Unteroffizier Martin Winkler shot down by a H-75A from GC II/5, the *Jagdflieger* force-landing his burning fighter. Badly wounded, Winkler died four days later.

As the first month of the war neared its end, I. and II./JG 53 continued to bring down the occasional enemy aircraft – four confirmed for I. *Gruppe* (including another balloon for 'Igel' Prestele) and six for II. *Gruppe*. Against this, II./JG 53 had recorded its first casualty when 6. *Staffel*'s Feldwebel Heinz Hellge was reportedly lost in action against Morane-Saulnier fighters over Bergzabern on 22 September. The previous day Hauptmann Dr Mix of I./JG 53 had claimed his second victory of World War 2 while engaging nine MS.406s from GC I/3 that were escorting two Potez reconnaissance aircraft from GAO 505. He subsequently recalled;

'Five aircraft of the *Gruppenstab* dodged about between the thunderclouds that covered the entire sector of the front. The *Kommandeur* discovered a French reconnaissance machine [a Potez 39 parasol-wing aircraft] below.

Four of us fired at it. The observer hung out of his seat half dead. Pieces flew from the wings, but the pilot managed to put his aircraft down near a French anti-aircraft position and we came away empty-handed. At the same instant the call came over the radio: "Fighters above!" I pulled up to the right and saw a Morane sitting behind a 109, firing. It had climbed so steeply that it now had to make a turn.

'Excellent! It turned to the right, directly in front of my guns. I fired into its fuselage from below and at once thick black smoke poured out. The Frenchman dived, my second burst following from behind and above. Following this the Morane went down in a steep dive, leaving a dense smoke trail, and finally crashed in a small wood. The adjutant radioed: "He's in the drink!"'

With the arrival of winter weather, combats began to decrease, as did the victories. By the end of 1939 I. *Gruppe* had claimed 28 aircraft and two balloons and II. *Gruppe* 13 aircraft and two balloons. However, one ex-*Legion Condor* pilot had been killed and another wounded – Oberfeldwebel Willbald Hein of 3. *Staffel* was killed in combat on 30 September 1939, just after shooting down his second aircraft of the war (to add to the four victories he claimed in Spain), while Oberleutnant Günther 'Schubla' Schulze-Blanck of 4. *Staffel* was wounded in combat that same day. The 30th had in fact seen the fiercest fighting yet over France. The day began with a solitary Potez 637 reconnaissance aircraft of GR II/52 falling to Hauptmann Günther *Freiherr* von Maltzahn, the *Kommandeur* of II. *Gruppe*, over the Saarbrücken area in the late morning. This was the first victory credited to future Oak Leaves *Experte* 'Henri' von Maltzahn.

Shortly after the demise of the Potez, which crash-landed in flames in France, a formation of five unescorted Battles of the RAF's No 150 Sqn approached the same Saarbrücken-Merzig sector on a high-altitude photographic reconnaissance mission. The British machines were intercepted by eight *Emils* of 2./JG 53 and all of them were destroyed. The first fell to the guns of *Staffelkapitän* Oberleutnant Rolf Pingel close to the target area. The last was chased 20 miles back into French territory by future ace Unteroffizier Josef Wurmheller, who riddled it with cannon and machine gun fire before breaking off the pursuit. 'Sepp' Wurmheller confidently claimed the Battle destroyed, as indeed it was. Although the pilot managed to get the crippled machine back to No 150 Sqn's airfield near Chalons, it burst into flames upon landing and was destroyed.

Pictured in front of the *Deutsche Forschungsansalt für Segelflug* (German Gliding Research Institute) hangar at Darmstadt-Griesheim, these five pilots of 2./JG 53 destroyed an entire formation of RAF Battles west of Saarbrücken on 30 September 1939. They are, from left to right, Unteroffizier Josef 'Sepp' Wurmheller, Unteroffizier Franz Kaiser, Oberleutnant Rolf Pingel (*Staffelkapitän*), Stabsfeldwebel Ignaz 'Igel' Prestele and Unteroffizier Hans Kornatz. All of them would subsequently become aces (*John Weal*)

Other elements of the *Geschwader* did not fare so well against Hawk H-75A and MS.406 fighters that same 30 September. Four pilots were killed and a fifth belly-landed his damaged 'White 10' (of 1. *Staffel*) near Wiesbaden

During the course of two further engagements later that same afternoon, pilots of 3. and 5. *Staffeln* were credited with another seven French aircraft destroyed, taking the *Geschwader*'s total for the day to 13. These victories had come at a price, however, for six Bf 109Es had been destroyed (and three more damaged) and four pilots killed. These fighters had fallen to French H-75As and MS.406s.

A number of ex-*Legion Condor* pilots in I. and II./JG 53 were slowly starting to build on their scores from Spain, namely Oberleutnante Hans-Karl Mayer (1), Wolfgang Lippert (1), Rolf Pingel (2), Rudolf Goy (1)

Officers of the newly activated III./JG 53 at Wiesbaden-Erbenheim in the autumn of 1939. They are, from left to right, Leutnant Friedrich-Karl Müller, an unidentified hauptmann of ground personnel (dark collar tabs), Hauptmann Werner Mölders (*Gruppenkommandeur*) and Oberleutnant Hans von Hahn (*Staffalkapitän* 8./JG 53). All three pilots would enjoy great aerial success in 1940 (*John Weal*)

Members of the RAD (Reich Labour Service) prepare to clear the wreckage of what is reported to be Hauptmann Werner Mölders' second kill, a Blenheim IV of No 18 Sqn that he brought down over the Moselle on 30 October 1939. The aeroplane, flown by Flg Off Denis Elliot, crashed near Küsserath, nine miles east-northeast of Trier. Its three-man crew was killed (*John Weal*)

and Heinz Bretnütz (2), Oberfeldwebeln Heinz Grimmling (2) and Ignaz Prestele (3) and Hauptmann Lothar von Janson (1). One name conspicuous by its absence from this list was Hauptmann Werner Mölders, who, after claiming just a solitary victory with 1. *Staffel*, had been given command of the newly formed III./JG 53 on 18 September 1939. He had in turn handed his old *Staffel* over to his good friend, and future ace, Oberleutnant Hans-Karl 'Mayer-Ast' Mayer. By the end of 1939 Mölders had shot down two more aircraft, including III. *Gruppe*'s first victory in the form of a Blenheim IV of No 18 Sqn on 30 October 1939. Making the most of a break in the weather, he was at the head of the *Gruppenschwarm*, leading 12 *Emils* of 9. *Staffel* on patrol, when enemy reconnaissance aircraft were reported in the Bitburg-Merzig area.

'I noticed flak activity near Trier,' Mölders later recalled. 'I closed up to within 50 m of the enemy machine undetected and could quite clearly see the British roundels. I opened fire from the shortest range possible. There was no return fire from the rear gunner and the left engine emitted a thick cloud of white smoke, which quickly changed to black. As I pulled up alongside it, the aircraft was completely on fire. I observed a parachute, but it appeared to be smouldering. The Blenheim crashed near Klüsserath, on the River Moselle.'

The Blenheim IV, flown by Flg Off Denis Elliot, crashed near Küsserath, nine miles east-northeast of Trier. Its three-man crew was killed.

With the *Gruppenkommandeur* having broken their duck, the pilots of III./JG 53 subsequently claimed seven of the *Geschwader*'s eleven November successes. These included

a Potez 63.11 of GR II/22 and two
Potez 637s of GR I/33 brought
down west of Saarbrücken on
7 November, one of which provided
a first for future *Ritterkreuz mit
Schwerten* (Knight's Cross with
Swords) recipient Oberleutnant
Wolf-Dietrich Wilcke, *Kapitän* of
7. *Staffel*. The only victories in
December 1939 followed the first
ever engagement between German
and British fighters in World War 2.
On the 22nd, elements of III./JG 53
were providing top cover for a pair

of Dornier Do 17 reconnaissance machines some 12 miles inside French
airspace when they spotted three enemy fighters far below. Werner Mölders
was again in the lead as the 'Emils' dived on the apparently unsuspecting
trio. He put an accurate burst of fire into the aircraft on the left – initially
identifying it as a French Morane – which went down in flames to crash
close to a village.

The first victory bar for a 9. *Staffel* pilot is
applied to the tail of the Bf 109E flown by
future ace Leutnant Jakob Stoll after he
downed an ANF Le Mureaux 117 parasol-
wing all-metal monoplane of GAO 2/506
on 6 November 1939. It was one of two
such aircraft destroyed by 9./JG 53 that
day during a photo-reconnaissance
mission of the defences at Metz

Shortly afterwards future ace Oberleutnant Hans von Hahn, the *Kapitän*
of 8. *Staffel*, sent a second enemy machine spinning and tumbling into
a nearby forest, where it too burst into flames on impact. He described
how he claimed his first victory as follows;

'Near Trier sighted numerous contrails in the direction of Diedenhofen.
My machine grew ever larger in the Revi [gunsight], and I thought of
"Vati's" [Mölders'] order. "Get in close and then let him sit firmly in the
aiming reticule." Now I pressed all the triggers. The Morane entered
a gentle turn, and at that moment took a cannon hit beneath the cockpit.
The burst of machine gun fire must have hit the pilot. The crate stood on
its nose, a jet of flame shot high, and then the enemy plunged into the
depths like a fiery comet. There was another flash of fire when he crashed.'

The two fighters, both of which had gone down about ten miles northeast
of Metz, were not MS.406s, however, but Hurricanes of the RAF's

Hauptmann Werner Mölders (foreground
right, facing camera) regales air- and
groundcrew of his *Gruppenstab* with
details of his latest encounter with the
enemy – possibly that which resulted in
his third victory, a No 73 Sqn Hurricane
claimed over French territory on
22 December 1939 (*John Weal*)

No 73 Sqn. Their pilots, Sgts R M Perry and J Winn, were both killed. Apart from this one action, there was little aerial activity in December.

It had been a slow but successful start to the war for JG 53, which by now had formally adopted the name 'Pik-As', its aircraft sporting an 'Ace of Spades' badge set in a diamond on either side of their cowlings.

JANUARY TO 9 MAY 1940 – A SLOW START

With winter refusing to release its icy grip, the first two months of 1940 were almost entirely uneventful for JG 53. However, the year started badly for 1. *Staffel*'s future ace Leutnant Hans Ohly, whose first operational flight had taken place on 30 December 1939. His second, three days later, was almost his last. After taking off at 1347 hrs on a patrol over the frontline, 1. *Staffel* was attacked by H-75As of GC II/5 and came off worse, with Leutnant Walter Rupp landing his damaged fighter back at Wiesbaden-Erbenheim and Ohly, who had been wounded in combat, possibly with Lt Robert Huvet, force-landing his fighter near St Wendel. His wounds prevented him from returning to flying duties until 7 May 1940, just three days before the start of the Battle of France.

Between January and 9 May 1940 I. *Gruppe* recorded just two victories. The first of these went to *Legion Condor* ace Oberleutnant Wolfgang Lippert, *Staffelkapitän* of 3./JG 53, on 7 April 1940 when he shot down Flg Off George Brotchie of No 73 Sqn southwest of Diedenhofen. The RAF pilot bailed out over Thionville, suffering splinter wounds to his right knee. In the same combat Flg Off Peter Ayerst of No 73 Sqn accounted for Feldwebel Erwin Weiss of 4./JG 53, whose Bf 109E-1 crashed six miles southeast of Diedenhofen, killing its pilot.

The only success for III. *Gruppe* during this lean period was a single MS.406 brought down south of Perl by Leutnant Walter Radlick of the *Gruppenstab* on 10 January. In March, however, activity in the air finally began to pick up for III./JG 53 again as the weather slowly improved. III. *Gruppe* – its individual *Staffeln* now operating on a rotational basis out of Trier-Euren, hard by the Luxembourg border – took a limited but steady toll of French and British machines throughout the month. By its end the *Gruppe* had added nine more victories to its collective total, with *Kommandeur* Hauptmann Werner Mölders having doubled his existing score to six in the process.

By contrast, II./JG 53 crammed all of its March successes into one frenetic ten-minute engagement on the last day of the month. It was mid-afternoon when 20 *Emils* of Hauptmann von Maltzahn's *Gruppe* chanced upon a disorganised formation of 11 MS.406s of GC III/7 southwest of Saargemünd. Choosing their moment, the Messerschmitts pounced between St Avold and Hambach, claiming six

Officers of III. *Gruppe* come together for a group photograph in the early spring of 1940. They are, front row, from left to right, Leutnant Josef Volk (9. *Staffel*, two victories, PoW from 11 November 1940), Oberleutnant Heinz Wittenberg (*Stab.*, two victories, survived), Hauptmann Werner Mölders, Leutnant Walter Radlick (*Stab.*, four victories, killed on 2 October 1940) and Leutnant Georg Claus (*Stab.*, 18 victories, killed on 11 November 1940). Middle row, from left to right, Oberleutnant Otto Boenigk (9. *Staffelkapitän*, one victory, survived), Dr Söstmann, Oberleutnant Wolf-Dietrich Wilcke (7. *Staffelkapitän*, 162 victories, killed on 23 March 1944), Leutnant Hans Riegel (7. *Staffel*, one victory, killed on 6 September 1940), Leutnant Jakob Stoll (8. *Staffel*, 13 victories, killed on 17 October 1940) and Leutnant Horst von Wegemann (9. *Staffel*, one victory, killed on 10 March 1941). Rear row, from left to right, Leutnant Ernst Panthen, (8. *Staffel*, three victories, survived), Leutnant Heinz Kunert (8. *Staffel*, nine victories, killed 8 September 1940), Stabzahlmeister Ehrhardt, Leutnant Hans Fleitz (8. *Staffel*, three victories, killed on 3 June 1940) and Oberleutnant Hans von Hahn (8. *Staffelkapitän*, 34 victories, survived)

of the eleven French fighters shot down. Four MS.406s were destroyed and another three damaged, with one pilot being killed and four wounded or injured. All of these victories were credited to future aces, with one MS.406 providing 'Henri' von Maltzahn with his second success. Another was a first for future Oak Leaves wearer Leutnant Gerhard Michalski of the *Gruppenstab*, while Oberleutnant Heinz Bretnütz – the *Kapitän* of 6. *Staffel* – was credited with a brace, which took his score to four. Unteroffizier Werner Kauffmann (4. *Staffel*) and Feldwebel Albrecht Baun (6. *Staffel*) also claimed an MS.406 apiece. All were to shoot down a minimum of five aircraft before the end of 1940, and three of them would be awarded the *Ritterkreuz* (Knight's Cross).

Bretnütz was up on patrol again that same evening when he claimed a Wellington, which, although confirmed at the time, was not substantiated by British records.

During April it was clear that final preparations for the invasion of France were nearing completion, and that same month JG 53 began to take delivery of its first more powerfully armed Bf 109E-4s. And the *Geschwader's* strength was further bolstered by the temporary attachment of another *Gruppe* – Major Wolf-Heinrich von Houwald's recently formed and as yet unblooded III./JG 52, which took up residence at Mannheim-Sandhofen alongside II./JG 53 on 6 April.

LEFT
Wearing a fur-lined flying suit, Hauptmann Werner Mölders of III./JG 53 climbs out of the cockpit of his reserve Bf 109E at Trier following an uneventful patrol in the early spring of 1940

RIGHT
When this photograph was taken in the spring of 1940, Hauptmann Günther von Maltzahn was *Gruppenkommandeur* of II./JG 53 – a position he filled from 18 August 1939 through to 8 October 1940, when he was made *Kommodore* of JG 53. He had previously been the *Staffelkapitän* of 6./JG 53 from June 1937. All 67 of victories came with the 'Pik-As' between 20 September 1939 and 4 January 1943, and he survived the war

With the weak spring sun having finally arrived and his work done, the crew chief (at far left) of 'Yellow 10' grabs the opportunity to doze on the wingroot of his charge. This machine was one of two Bf 109Es assigned to Oberleutnant Heinz Bretnütz (the other aircraft was 'Yellow 11'), the *Staffelkapitän* of 6./JG 53 at Mannheim-Sandhofen. On the original print three white victory bars can be made out on the tailfin above the parachute – Bretnütz's third victim was an MS.406 claimed on the afternoon of 31 March 1940, and his fourth another of the same ilk just two minutes later (*John Weal*)

Hauptmann Werner Mölders' Bf 109E at Trier in March 1940, showing five victory bars on its tail. The aeroplane displays the two-tone green finish favoured by III./JG 53 for much of the 'Phoney War' period and sports pre-war style national insignia. The last of the five victory bars displayed on the tailfin represents a French MS.406 brought down near Metz on 3 March 1940

No 73 Sqn had eight run-ins with JG 53 during the 'Phoney War', and came off worst on nearly each occasion. These two pilots were shot down by I. *Gruppe* in April 1940, Flg Off George Brotchie (left) falling to Oberleutnant Wolfgang Lippert on the 7th and Plt Off Peter Walker being claimed by Oberleutnant Hans-Karl Mayer on the 21st. Both Brotchie and Walker suffered splinter wounds from cannon shells when attacked, hence their hospitalisation

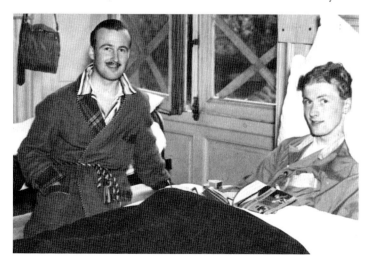

In the air, the *Geschwader* was experiencing something of a lull. Another clash with No 73 Sqn's Hurricanes on 7 April resulted in a single kill for 3./JG 53's *Staffelkapitän*, Oberleutnant Wolfgang Lippert – who identified his opponent as a Spitfire – but also led to the loss of Feldwebel Erwin Weiss of 4. *Staffel*, as previously noted. Weiss thus had the dubious honour of being the first pilot of JG 53 to fall victim to the RAF, five others having previously been killed in action against the *Armée de l'Air*. Exactly two weeks later, on 21 April, JG 53 and No 73 Sqn met again. This time Oberleutnant Hans-Karl Mayer had no difficulty in recognising the British fighter he claimed northwest of Merzig as a Hurricane. It was Mayer's second success since taking over from Werner Mölders as *Kapitän* of 1. *Staffel*. His combat report for the mission read as follows;

'Mission – fighter sweep in the Trier-Pirmasens area. In the Merzig area I noticed heavy German anti-aircraft fire and saw a twin-engined machine with strong fighter escort. Before I attacked, my covering *Schwarm* was attacked from above by four to six Curtisses. At first I flew some way to the east, gained height and climbed above two Hurricanes, behind which I was able to position myself without being seen. When the two Hurricanes turned, I moved into a good firing position close (80 m) behind the higher one. The first hits from my cannon fire caused pieces to fly from the machine. I observed no more evasive action after the second burst. The aircraft slowly dropped its right wing and began to go down. I descended to search the lower altitudes for enemy aircraft. As I did so I saw a cloud of smoke near a large wood where an aircraft had crashed and exploded. I had not watched it go down as I was searching the airspace around me for aircraft.

'The air battle had immediately broken up into individual combats, as a second 109 *Staffel*, which was flying somewhat lower, had contacted the enemy first. I had to break off the air battle as the *Staffel* had already been in the air for one hour and ten minutes.'

Mayer's victim was Plt Off Peter Walker, who force-landed with splinter wounds to his shoulder in French-held territory. Mayer had fired a total of 77 20 mm cannon and 123 7.9 mm machine gun rounds at Walker's Hurricane. His *Rottenflieger* (wingman), Unteroffizier Ludwig Reibel, who would later become an ace, reported seeing black smoke coming from the British fighter before it dropped away six to nine miles west of Merzig, this also being witnessed by Leutnant Ernst-Albrecht Schulz, who was flying behind Mayer, and Major Richard Kraut, *Gruppenkommandeur* of I./JG 76. Kraut's *Gruppe* had been escorting an Hs 126 on a reconnaissance sortie when it had been bounced by No 73 Sqn, losing Feldwebel Leopold Wyhlidal of 2./JG 76 to Sqn Ldr James More near Merzig. These victories were the second of the war for Lippert and Mayer, both of whom would account for many more aircraft later in 1940, earning them the *Ritterkreuz* in September of that year.

From 1 January to 10 May 1940, III./JG 53 proved to be the most successful *Gruppe* within the *Geschwader*, its pilots claiming to have shot down 15 aircraft – all but one of them being single-engined fighters. Mölders' log book shows he flew five combat missions in January, three in February, 18 in March and ten in April 1940, by which time he had shot down two Hurricanes, two MS.406s and a 'Hawk 36', taking his score to nine. He had been credited with three of the four victories scored by III. *Gruppe* in April. The fourth – a No 73 Sqn Hurricane sent down by Mölders' wingman and future ace, Feldwebel Franz Gawlick, on 23 April, would prove to be JG 53's last victory of the 'Phoney War'. Just minutes earlier Mölders had himself claimed his final success of this period. After taking off from Wiesbaden at 1030 hrs, he and Gawlick had bounced two Hurricanes and both of them went down. Mölders' victim was Sgt Ken Campbell, whose account of what happened is very graphic;

'Whilst on patrol over the German lines at what we called Hell Fire Corner – the junction of Germany, France and Luxembourg – together with Sgt Tom Pyne, we were attacked by nine Me 109s. We had turned away from the German lines and Tom had lagged behind when I suddenly heard him say, "109s! Look out!"

'Turning quickly, I saw a gaggle of aircraft about half-a-mile away and opened up to join my comrade. As I was flying straight and level I received a burst of shells over my port wing. I banked to starboard and back again, seeing a 109 overshoot underneath me. Foolishly I straightened up again, heading for where I thought my friend was. I then received another burst of shells at the rear of my aircraft from another 109. I carried out the same manoeuvre and he overshot underneath. Once more I straightened out, and immediately I received another burst in the cockpit. This burst hit my legs and severed my throttle controls.

Oberleutnant Hans-Karl Mayer took over 1. *Staffel* from Werner Mölders when the latter was given command of the newly formed III./JG 53 on 30 September 1939. Also an ace from the conflict in Spain, Mayer would be credited with 22 victories between 5 November 1939 and 15 September 1940 to add to the eight he had claimed with *Jagdgruppe* 88 in 1938. One of the tallest pilots in the Luftwaffe at that time, Mayer was a highly effective and well-respected *Staffelkapitän* and, later, *Gruppenkommandeur*. Unteroffizier Werner Karl, who served with him in 1. *Staffel* recalled, 'To me, Hauptmann Mayer was the most remarkable personality; he was exemplary in every respect. He was so tall, he used to cram himself into his cockpit and when on missions used twice as much oxygen than the rest of us'

'Finding that I could not out-turn the 109 with my throttle jammed wide open, I tried to shake him by cutting my ignition switches on the turn and switching them on again as I banked round again. This proved of no avail as there were now at least three 109s behind me [and] whichever way I turned I received a burst of fire. Then the gravity tank in front of the cockpit was hit and burst into flames, which covered the whole of the cockpit. Instinctively, I turned my face away from the wall of flames and released my hood and emergency panel. Without waiting to release my radio or oxygen connections, I threw myself out of the cockpit sideways. I was at approximately 26,000 ft. I suppose the shock, burns, etc., made me weak because as I threw myself out I felt my senses going. Instinct plus practice made my hand reach for the "D" ring and pull it.'

Flg Off Edgar 'Cobber' Kain' (left) and Sgt Ken Campbell of No 73 Sqn also tangled with JG 53 during the 'Phoney War'. New Zealander Kain was downed twice, on 2 March, when he claimed a Bf 109 destroyed – none were actually lost – before being forced to crash-land after being attacked by Hauptmann Werner Mölders, and 24 days later, when he claimed two more Bf 109s destroyed – one returned to base damaged. It appears that Mölders got him the second time too, although the German ace claimed he had downed an MS.406. Between 8 November 1939 and 27 May 1940 Kain was credited with 16 aircraft destroyed and one damaged. He was killed in a flying accident on 6 June 1940. Ken Campbell was also shot down by Mölders, on 23 April, bailing out of his blazing fighter at 26,000 ft and landing in France

Campbell landed on the French side of the frontline and, having convinced French soldiers he was not German, was rushed to the nearest hospital at Thionville. Meanwhile, Tom Pyne managed to crash-land at Sierck-les-Bains, wounded in the shoulder, and his Hurricane was written off. Pyne was subsequently killed in action on 14 May 1940.

These final victories were almost retribution for III./JG 53, which had locked horns a number of times with Hurricanes in March and April 1940. For example, on 22 March Flt Lt Reg Lovett of No 73 Sqn damaged the Bf 109E of Feldwebel Arthur Weigelt of 8. *Staffel* (who would be mortally injured in an accident just under a month later), and then on 20 April Leutnant Fritz Sievers of 7./JG 53 was shot down and killed by Flt Lt Peter 'Johnnie' Walker of No 1 Sqn.

The combat of 23 April proved to be the last of the 'Phoney War' for JG 53. Werner Mölders recorded just three more operational flights before Germany invaded France, Luxembourg and the Low Countries on 10 May, after which the war became far more intense and combat experience was vital if one wanted to survive.

Mölders' nearest rival in JG 53 in terms of aerial victories during this period was Oberleutnant Heinz Bretnütz of 6. *Staffel* with five.

Since the British and French declarations of war on 3 September 1939 the *Geschwader* had destroyed 73 enemy aircraft at a cost of 12 of its own pilots – seven killed or missing in action and five lost through accidents and to other causes.

CHAPTER TWO

BATTLE OF FRANCE

As German forces rolled over the border just before dawn on 10 May 1940, JG 53 was immediately in action. Leutnant Hans Ohly of 1. *Staffel* reported getting airborne from Darmstadt at 0720 hrs to relocate to the forward airfield of Kirchberg, near Simmern, after which he was flown back to Darmstadt by a Focke-Wulf Fw 58 and began ferrying another five Bf 109Es over the next 24 hours. He did not fly his first operational sortie until 12 May 1940. The only victory on the first day of the Battle of France by I. *Gruppe* went to Oberleutnant Wolfgang Lippert when he shot down a Curtiss southwest of Metz at 1355 hrs. This was possibly a Bloch MB.152 of GC II/8 that crashed at Jaulny, killing its pilot, Capt Adrien Astier.

An hour later Feldwebel Stefan Litjens of 4./JG 53 claimed his first confirmed success – an unidentified Curtiss near Metz. His first claimed victory – an MS.406 west of Saarbrücken on 7 April 1940 – was not confirmed, but it now appears that it might have been a Morane-Saulnier of GC III/3 that crashed at Morhange, killing Capt André Richard.

10 May was not particularly successful for 1. *Staffel*, as Gefreiter Ludwig Reibel suffered a mid-air collision with Leutnant Walter Rupp. The latter's Bf 109E-4 lost its tail and he was forced to bail out, his injuries preventing him from re-joining I./JG 53 until September 1940. Reibel managed to force-land his Bf 109E-3 at Serrig, the fighter being badly damaged as a result. That same day Unteroffizier Josef Groten crash-landed his fighter due

Future ace Feldwebel Stefan Litjens of 4./JG 53 flew Bf 109E-4 Wk-Nr 1244 'White 5' from Mannheim-Sandhofen during the spring of 1940, claiming several victories in it

to causes unknown, being slightly injured in the process. He did the same again on 14 May and three days later during a transfer flight, but on that occasion his injuries were more serious. Groten's name does not reappear until 3 March 1945, when he was reported missing while flying with 1./JG 3. Finally, Leutnant Gerhard Carnier of 2. *Staffel* was shot down on 10 May 1940 by Adj de Montgolfier of GC II/5. Captured, having been wounded in the engagement, Carnier was released after the French surrender and joined 9./JG 51. He was later killed on operations on 30 September 1940.

No victories were achieved by III. *Gruppe* on 10 May 1940, despite Mölders flying three 'Freie Jagd' (Free Hunt) sorties in the Diedenhofen/Metz area – the first from 0555 hrs to 0715 hrs, the second from 1250 hrs to 1415 hrs and the last from 1445 hrs to 1605 hrs. The following day he flew another three 'Freie Jagd' in the Longwy/Carignau area, again without incident.

On 11 May 1./JG 53 had better luck, three of its ex-*Legion Condor* pilots, Oberleutnant Hans-Karl Mayer, Oberfeldwebel Heinz Grimmling and Oberfeldwebel Alfred 'Molinero' Muller, each claiming an MS.406 without loss. Mayer's combat report for this action read as follows;

'Mission – Rendezvous with bomber units near Longwy. We passed friendly aircraft heading home while en route. While loitering as per our orders, at 7.40 am I sighted a formation of bombers from Saarbrücken heading in the direction of Pont-a-Mousson at 7000 m. Behind the He 111 *Staffel* were three enemy fighters, which we attacked at once. Oberfeldwebel Grimmling was the first to open fire. I saw the entire tail section fly away. Meanwhile, more Moranes and Curtisses arrived (about ten aircraft). I made two more attacks and got in a good burst at the second Morane. Pieces of the machine flew away as the burst struck home and the pilot tried to climb away to the left. I continued to fire as he did so. I moved up close beside the machine and saw the pilot hanging half out of his cockpit, his head completely shattered. The aircraft then slowly rolled over one wing and went down.'

These successes took Mayer's, Grimmling's and Muller's individual scores to three, three and one, respectively, with no losses being suffered by I. *Gruppe*. Oberleutnant Heinz Bretnütz of 6. *Staffel* achieved the only kill of the day for II. *Gruppe*, his sixth of the war so far.

Again, on 12 May, Mölders recorded an inconclusive scramble to intercept 31 enemy fighters, followed by two uneventful 'Freie Jagds' in the Sedan-Montmédy-Longwy area. This last mission saw Feldwebel Hans Galubinski of 7. *Staffel* getting III. *Gruppe*'s first victory of the Battle of France – a Potez 63 – and his first of the war. In the space of just three weeks, 24-year-old Galubinski would bring down nine aircraft. However, on 6 June 1940 he was shot down and taken prisoner. Released after the French capitulation, Galubinski rejoined 7./JG 53, but his next success did not come until 22 June 1941. By 9 September 1941 his score had risen to 28. Still with 7./JG 53, he was awarded the *Deutsches Kreuz* in Gold in July 1942, but it appears that Galubinski then became a fighter instructor, as on 13 January 1944 (the day after his 28th birthday and still holding the rank of Oberfeldwebel) he was shot down while flying with I./JG 101 when his elderly Bf 109E was bounced by Hawker Typhoons of No 198 Sqn flown by either Sqn Ldr John Bryan and Flg Off Harold Freeman or by Flg Off John Niblett, who between them claimed two Bf 109s near Rosières. Concidentally, all three Allied pilots were

Feldwebel Hans Galubinski of 7./JG 53 was credited with eight aircraft destroyed (and a ninth unconfirmed) between 12 May and 6 June 1940, although he was himself shot down on the latter date by Adj Jean Crocq of GC II/1. Assigned to 7./JG 53, Galubinski and his *Staffel* had taken on 12 MB.152s near Soissons. Three Bloch fighters were destroyed, although Galubinski was in turn shot down after claiming two of his French opponents. The ace was fired on by furious civilians as he descended beneath his parachute, being seriously wounded by shotgun pellets prior to his capture. (*Conrad*)

killed over Normandy later the same year. Galubinski was killed when his aircraft crashed at Caix, 15 miles east-southeast of Amiens.

Returning to May 1940, on the 13th JG 53 again saw very little action, with I. *Gruppe* claiming two victories without loss. Although Mölders completed two uneventful 'Freie Jagd' with III./JG 53, II. *Gruppe* recorded three confirmed and two unconfirmed victories at noon, including the first for Oberleutnant Kurt Brändle of 4. *Staffel*. His victim was possibly the H-75A of GC I/5 flown by Czech pilot Lt Adolf Vrana, who was shot down near Harricourt.

7. *Staffel*'s most successful pilots pose for the camera at the conclusion of the French campaign, having each just been awarded with the *Eisernes Kreuz* first class. They are, from left to right, Oberfeldwebel Franz Götz (who was credited with five confirmed and two unconfirmed victories during the campaign), Leutnant Heinz Altendorf (four victories) and Unteroffizier Hermann Neuhoff (seven victories). All three survived the war, with Götz and Neuhoff subsequently receiving the *Ritterkreuz*. Like Altendorf, Neuhoff was forced down behind enemy lines and captured – he crash-landed on Malta on 10 April 1942 (*Helm*)

Vrana survived, went on to fly with the RAF and survived the war. Although this would prove to be both Brändle's first and last kill of the Battle of France (he was injured in an accident on 26 May and did not claim his next success until 11 August), by the end of 1940 his score has risen to six. His tally stood at 170 victories by the time of his death on 3 November 1943, Brändle having been awarded the *Ritterkreuz mit Eichenlaub* (Knight's Cross with Oak Leaves) prior to his demise.

The first four days of the Battle of France were very much the lull before the storm for JG 53, as on 14 May I. *Gruppe* was credited with an astonishing 35 victories, III. *Gruppe* claimed seven more (albeit three were unconfirmed), and II. *Gruppe* achieved three unconfirmed victories. These successes were prompted by the rapidity of the German advance, the French defensive line along the Meuse failing and the RAF carrying out a series of near-suicidal bombing attacks with its highly vulnerable Battles and Blenheims.

Leutnant Hans Ohly of 1. *Staffel* records being scrambled from Kirchberg at 0625 hrs and patrolling the Kreuznach-Karlsruhe area without incident. After landing at 0730 hrs he took off on a second patrol at 1100 hrs, landing at Trier and then flying back to Kirchberg at 1414 hrs. During this last patrol, 2. and 3. *Staffeln* were involved in a dogfight with Bloch MB.151s south of Sedan, claiming five and one destroyed, respectively – Hauptmann Rolf Pingel was credited with two of them.

Just after this combat III. *Gruppe* completed a 'Freie Jagd' in the Sedan area, again without incident, although an earlier flight that day had seen two pilots of 7. *Staffel*, Unteroffiziere Hans-Georg Schulte and Hermann Neuhoff, claim an MS.406 each. Both pilots would enjoy more successes in the months to come. And at last Mölders managed to get his first victory of the Battle of France when, at 1630 hrs, he was involved in a dogfight with 16 Hurricanes and shot one down for his tenth success of the war. His victim was believed to be Sgt Leon Dibden of No 73 Sqn, whose Hurricane crashed and burned out in a wood at La Haie Colette, just north of Noirval. Dibden was killed, the RAF pilot being buried in the local churchyard the following day. Ten years later, almost to the day, his body was exhumed and now lies at Choloy.

However, while III. *Gruppe* was claiming two Hurricanes, 1. *Staffel* was having a field day southwest of Sedan. Engaged on a 'Freie Jagd' in support of two formations of Ju 87 Stukas attacking targets in Sedan, it came across

Battles and Blenheims of No 71 Wing (Nos 105, 114, 139 and 150 Sqns), together with their escort. In the space of 22 minutes 1./JG 53 claimed two Hurricanes, six Battles and six Blenheims destroyed. The first RAF aeroplane to fall was a Hurricane claimed by Hans-Karl Mayer, who, in just 12 minutes, claimed an additional two Battles and two Blenheims. Combat reports were understandably terse, as Meyer's account for his first victory reveals;

'The *Staffel* was flying at 5000 m, passing a group of Stukas some 1500 m below us, when we were attacked by six Hurricanes. The *Deckungsschwarm* [Lookout *Schwarm*, consisting of Leutnant Alfred Zeis, Feldwebel Alfred Stark, Unteroffizier Ludwig Reibel and Unteroffizier Heinrich Höhnisch] immediately engaged them. I led the rest of the *Staffel* down to protect the Stukas, which were coming under attack from other enemy fighters. I shot down a Hurricane, which crashed and burned on impact.'

Mayer reported that the Hurricane pilot must have been killed by his burst of fire, and that he then went after, and shot down, four more RAF aircraft. He fired a total of 120 20 mm cannon and 560 7.9 mm machine gun rounds in the process. His first victim is thought to have been Sgt Dennis Allen of No 3 Sqn, whose Hurricane plunged into dense forest three miles northeast of Villers-Cernay, taking him with it.

The engagement proved to be a one-sided slaughter, with Mayer and his *Rottenflieger*, Hans Ohly, each downing a Blenheim, Mayer going for the right-hand one of a pair and Ohly the left-hand one. Both quickly hit the ground in flames. After this, Ohly shot down a second Blenheim and a Battle, the latter crash-landing on fire. Unteroffizier Heinrich Höhnisch accounted for a Hurricane and two Battles (his first three victories of the war), the future ace describing the Hawker fighter's demise in his combat report as follows;

'I was flying as the third man in Leutnant Zeis' *Schwarm*. At 4.20 pm enemy fighters were sighted above us. As I was forced away from the *Schwarm* at that moment, I moved off to the side and climbed above the aircraft now locked in combat. Suddenly, below me and to the right, I saw a Hurricane close behind a Bf 109 of our *Staffel*. As I was in an extremely favourable position to attack, I half-rolled and dived into position behind the Hurricane and shot it down in flames from 100-500 m. The Hurricane then went spinning down in flames.'

Other victories went to Unteroffizier Ludwig Reibel (a Blenheim) and Leutnant Ernst-Albrecht Schulz (a Battle).

The combat was not totally one-sided, however, as Hurricanes of No 1 Sqn managed to intercept 1./JG 53, shooting down former *Legion Condor* pilot Oberfeldwebel Walter Grimmling – it is believed the aircraft downed by Höhnisch had attacked Grimmling moments earlier. His Bf 109E-1 crashed at Fond Givonne, Illy, between Sedan and Bouillon, Grimmling initially being buried alongside the remains

Oberleutnant Hans-Karl Mayer (third from left) and pilots of his 1. *Staffel* enjoy the sun at Douzy during the brief hiatus between Operations *Yellow* and *Red*, the two-part conquest of France. The French campaign was very much the calm before the storm for 1./JG 53, with five of these pilots having either been killed or captured in the seven weeks from late August to mid-October 1940. They are, from left to right, Leutnant Alfred Zeis (PoW from 5 October 1940), Unteroffizier Heinrich Höhnisch (PoW from 9 September 1940), Oberleutnant Hans-Karl Mayer (killed on 17 October 1940), Leutnant Ernst-Albrecht Schulz (survived), Unteroffizier Herbert Tzschoppe (PoW from 15 September 1940) and Feldwebel Heinrich Bezner (killed on 26 August 1940)

of his fighter. He was posthumously promoted to leutnant. Two more aircraft, flown by Unteroffizier Josef Groten and Unteroffizier Herbert Tzschoppe, were damaged by No 1 Sqn and, short on fuel, force-landed. Tzschoppe's aircraft was written off, but not before he managed to liberate the control column as a souvenir (he still had it when interviewed by the author decades later). Oberleutnant Wilfried Balfanz of *Stab. I./JG 53* was also shot down and wounded, and it is possible that another fighter force-landed short of fuel without injury to its pilot.

There was one more victory for 1. *Staffel*, which also resulted in the death of the victorious pilot, Feldwebel Alfred Stark, another ex-*Legion Condor* pilot. Stark was seen by Leutnant Ernst-Albrecht Schulz and Unteroffizier Heinrich Höhnisch attacking a Blenheim believed to be from No 139 Sqn and flown by Sgt N E Brady. Stark got too close to the doomed bomber (which was abandoned by its crew), and when it exploded after crashing into woods near La Cassine his Bf 109E-4 apparently lost its starboard wingtip. Stark limped off in a southwesterly direction, but it is believed that he soon lost control of his fighter and it crashed at La Gravière, near Doux, killing him in the process. His body was never recovered and today he is still listed as missing, even though, when a Bf 109 at that location was recovered in 2002 and human remains were found (as well as the remains of a 'Pik-As' badge), they were not identified. Stark was credited with his first and only kill of the war, the 28th for 1. *Staffel* and the 88th for I. *Gruppe*, to go with the one he achieved in Spain.

There were other claims made by I. *Gruppe* in the same combat. Three went to *Stab. I./JG 53* and one to Ignaz Prestelle, who had apparently been commissioned as an oberleutnant and who could have been flying with 1. *Staffel* at the time – the Battle he downed was his second victory of the war.

Despite having suffered extensive losses during these late afternoon missions, the RAF again attempted to blunt the German advance with an evening Blenheim raid between 1930 and 1945 hrs. This time it was the turn of 3./JG 53 to claim seven aircraft destroyed. The pilots involved identified their opponents as Vickers Wellingtons and Blenheims, but they were in fact all Blenheim IVs of Nos 21, 107 and 110 Sqns. No 21 Sqn suffered three aircraft shot down or written off, with three aircrew killed and four wounded, while No 110 Sqn lost five aircraft with four killed, four captured and three wounded. Leutnant Wolfgang Tonne was shot down and wounded after shooting down a Blenheim, but his wounds did not keep him off flying for long, as he shot down his second aircraft of the war on 9 June 1940. He did not get his third until 15 September 1940, and his fifth came on 26 April 1941 (this long delay between successes was probably not helped by his *Staffel* becoming the *Jabo* or fighter-bomber unit of I./JG 53 in September 1940). By the time of his death on 20 April 1943 he had shot down 120 aircraft and been awarded the *Ritterkreuz mit Eichenlaub*.

The totals for 14 May – dubbed the 'Day of the Fighters' by the Luftwaffe – were 35 victories for I. *Gruppe* with six fighters lost and one damaged, two pilots killed and two wounded; II. *Gruppe* claimed three, which were not confirmed, with no losses; and III. *Gruppe* claimed four confirmed and three unconfirmed, for one pilot killed. It had indeed been a highly successful day, with a number of pilots either adding to their score or, like Leutnant Wolfgang Tonne, getting their foot on the victory ladder.

The days that followed were understandably quieter in respect of claims, even if the pace was still quite frantic. However, the air battles were not as one-sided. Hans Ohly recorded 12 'Frontflug' for the next ten days, but no combats, his first action being at midday on 25 May. While on a 'Freie Jagd' in the Chalons-sur-Marne area Oberleutnant Hans-Karl Mayer led six aircraft down to attack 15 H-75As, his victim reportedly exploding. However, Oberfeldwebel Alfred Müller stated that he saw *two* aircraft hit the ground. It appears that the one attacked by Mayer had brought down a second French fighter. Two H-75As of GC II/4 are reported to have collided when attacked and to have crashed near Machault, killing Adj Pierre Villey and Sgt Francois Dietrich. Shortly before this, Dietrich had been credited with shooting down Unteroffizier Ludwig Reibel, who was captured unhurt and released at the end of June 1940. Mayer was credited with his ninth victory, while the second aircraft was credited to 1. *Staffel* as a whole.

No victories or losses were recorded by 2. *Staffel* during the same period, although 3. *Staffel* claimed a total of five successes, two of which were credited to Oberleutnant Wolfgang Lippert, bringing his tally to six.

During the period to 25 May II. *Gruppe* also enjoyed a modicum of success, claiming three victories (two to Oberleutnant Heinz Bretnütz, whose score now stood at eight, and one to Feldwebel Albrecht Baun, whose tally was now three). However, II. *Gruppe* almost lost its *Gruppenkommandeur* twice when, on 15 May, Hauptmann Günther von Maltzahn had to force-land at Dockendorf with a technical problem and, five days later, his fighter was slightly damaged in combat. Both times he was uninjured.

The most successful unit by far was Mölders' III. *Gruppe*, which recorded 20 confirmed and five unconfirmed victories, six of which went to Mölders, taking his score to 17. His log book records 20 missions. Only one pilot was lost in combat, on a day when Mölders was not flying – Oberleutnant Wolf-Dietrich Wilcke, *Staffelkapitän* of 7. *Staffel*, who was another ex-*Legion Condor* pilot. He had shot down nothing in Spain, and had only brought down three aircraft up to March 1940, and nothing so far in the Battle of France. On the afternoon of 18 May, in a combat with H-75As that saw two confirmed victories (for Unteroffizier Hermann Neuhoff and Feldwebel Hans Galubinski) and one unconfirmed (for Oberfeldwebel Franz Götz) for Wilcke's *Staffel*, it is believed that he fell victim to Sous-Lt Camille Plubeau of GC II/4. Wilcke bailed out and his fighter crashed near Rethel. Four days later, he was reported a prisoner of the French, but was released at the end of the Battle of France. Temporary leadership of 7. *Staffel* was now given to Leutnant Hans Riegel.

Wilcke was another JG 53 pilot who went on to do well. By the end of 1940 his score had risen to 13, and he had increased it to 155 by the time of his death in action on 22 March 1944. Wilcke was one of the few pilots to be awarded the *Ritterkreuz mit Schwertern*.

Fellow future ace Oberleutnant Hans von Hahn of III./JG 53 also enjoyed success during this period, as he recalled in his combat report from 21 May;

'Bomber escort to Paris. 8. *Staffel* expanded fighter escort. Very heavy haze. Finally, we reached the French fighter defence zone around Paris. Our friends were up in numbers. We first took on a group of Curtisses, which climbed up out of the haze. Following Vati's [Mölders'] Curtiss tactic, we stayed above, turned with them and waited for a favourable opportunity to attack.

The Curtisses took to their heels, only half a squadron giving battle. Leutnant [Ernst] Panthen and I each got one. Panthen chased another bumblebee like a madman and my *Staffel*, too, had fallen upon the rest of the enemy, and so I was alone in the French sky.

'I set course for home and came upon Leutnant Fleitz, also flying alone. Then a lone twin-engined machine, a LeO 45, came flying towards us. We turned our crates around and went after it. I approached from the left and below, and after my very first burst flames came from the crate's wing, fuselage and left engine. It dropped a wing and crashed. Fleitz was excited and shouted over the radio.

'We were scarcely back on course when we saw a group of fighters in front of us. As we got closer they turned out to be five Hurricanes. Because of the fuel situation there was time for only one pass. And it was a good one. A Hurricane caught fire and exploded in midair. Now it was time to get away – nose down, full throttle and away to the east at treetop height. The enemy followed, but I was faster. The distance between us grew slowly, and then I was away from the pack of hounds. I hopped around cheerfully on my parachute, at least as much as my safety harness allowed, and whistled to myself. After making three victory passes I landed with my last drops of gas. For the first time I was reproached by Vati: "Victory passes on the last drops of fuel are out, you!" My *Staffel* scored an additional six victories that day.'

On 27 May III. *Gruppe* again scored well after I. *Gruppe* had claimed three aircraft – one of which gave Rolf Pingel his sixth victory – the previous day. In two combats on the 27th, one in the morning and one in the afternoon, III./JG 53 claimed another ten aircraft destroyed, including two for Mölders, to take his score to 20. His log book records that he took off from La Selve at 0845 hrs, apparently leading 8. *Staffel*, and attacked 'six Blochs' nine miles southwest of Amiens. What happened next was recorded in his wartime biography *Mölders und seine Männer* (*Mölders and his Men*) written by Major Fritz von Forrell and first published in 1941;

'Like a sudden storm, we fall upon the completely unsuspecting enemy from above. I line my sights upon the right-hand man of the rear section. Leutnant [Ernst] Panthen takes the left, while Leutnant [Friedrich-Karl] Müller pulls ahead of us and aims for the section leader. I can see the blue-white-red stripes on their tails quite clearly – edge in closer, metre by metre, take careful aim and right on target! My cannon and machine gun rounds erupt in tiny flashes all over the enemy. Another French fighter destroyed.

'All around me, my Messerschmitts are doing their job. The second *Schwarm* has overtaken us and is engaging the enemy's leading section. Every Bloch has a 109 glued to its tail. The enemy fighters don't get the chance to fire a single shot. There, Leutnant [Heinz] Kunert's victim is going down in flames. Beneath me I count four explosions as machines hit the ground. The enemy leader is still twisting and turning in confusion, but I keep after him. He too explodes on impact with the ground, not far from where Kunert's opponent went in. The last Frenchman is so shot up by Leutnant Panthen that he is forced to belly-land.'

Leutnant Heinz Altendorf of 7. *Staffel* receives the *Eisernes Kreuz* second class from his *Gruppenkommandeur*, Hauptmann Werner Mölders, in late May 1940. Having claimed four victories during the campaign in France, Altendorf 'made ace' with a Blenheim destroyed on 8 September, followed by a Spitfire 12 days later. He was eventually shot down over Libya on 16 December 1941, spending the rest of the conflict as a PoW. Altendorf had by then been credited with 24 victories

Hauptmann Werner Mölders' Bf 109E-4 at La Selve on or about 27 May 1940, displaying 18 victory bars on its fin. Mölders shot down his 18th aircraft on 25 May and the next two 48 hours later, for which he was awarded the *Ritterkreuz*. This was probably the aircraft he was flying from La Selve when he was shot down by Sous-Lt René Pomier Layrargues in a D.520 of GC II/7 west of Compiègne on 5 June, by which time his tally of 25 victories in World War 2 made him the second most successful 'Pik-As' pilot of 1940

Records now show that III./JG 53 probably attacked Bloch MB.152s of GC II/8, which suffered two shot down with one pilot killed and another wounded, and one returning damaged, so it would appear that III. *Gruppe's* claims were somewhat optimistic on this occasion. Later that afternoon it was the turn of 7./JG 53, with five claims for MS.406s, an H-75A and a Caudron C.714, all in the Amiens area. Curiously, eight MS.406s were also destroyed in a strafing attack on Damblain airfield, which is nowhere near Amiens. Nevertheless, the successful pilots, Feldwebel Herbert Schramm, Leutnant Heinz Altendorf, Oberfeldwebel Franz Götz, Feldwebel Hans Galubinski and Unteroffizier Hermann Neuhoff, were each credited with victories. All would go on to shoot down five or more aircraft in the following weeks and months.

Later that day 2. *Staffel* claimed two Potez 631s (which can be linked to French losses), while 5. *Staffel* claimed three twin-engined aircraft off Calais that are now thought to have been Blenheim IVs of No 107 Sqn, two of which were reported lost.

By now Mölders had become the first German fighter pilot to have shot down 20 enemy aircraft, for which he was awarded the *Ritterkreuz* on 29 May 1940 – he was the first member of the Luftwaffe to receive this decoration. There were celebrations that night and, unsurprisingly, he did not fly on 30 May but did manage a single mission on the evening of the 31st, shooting down a LeO 451. On that day III. *Gruppe* claimed an amazing 12 enemy aircraft without loss, I. *Gruppe* was credited with three but II. *Gruppe* failed to score, and lost Oberfeldwebel Walter Czikowsky to return fire from a French aircraft he was attacking. He was killed when he crashed at Marqueglise.

By that time Operation *Yellow*, the first phase of the Wehrmacht's methodical conquest of France, was complete. The armoured spearheads that had burst out of the Ardennes forests had reached the English Channel, forcing Belgium to surrender on 28 May. The last British troops had been evacuated from Dunkirk. Northeast France was in German hands. Now the invaders could launch Operation *Red*, the assault against the remaining bulk of the French field armies south of the Rivers Somme and Aisne. However, before supporting the ground operations during this second stage of the *Blitzkrieg* in the west, the Luftwaffe mounted its one major strategic bombing raid of the campaign. Flown on 3 June, Operation *Paula* was aimed at the airfields, aircraft manufacturing plants and associated targets in the Greater Paris area. All three of JG 53's *Gruppen* were involved in *Paula*, escorting Do 17 bombers and flying 'Freie Jagd' missions to the south of the French capital.

The day netted the *Geschwader* a further 14 victories, including two more for Werner Mölders (taking him to 23). But two pilots were lost – one brought down by French anti-aircraft fire and another by an MS.406. Amongst those to enjoy success was Oberleutnant Hans von Hahn of III./JG 53, who wrote the following combat report after the operation;

'Escort mission to Paris. A lousy outfit of Do 17s which flew like fools. Proper protection was out of the question, for the bombers had spread out all over the sky. My *Staffel* and I stayed with a larger group. When we reached Meaux the French came at us from all sides with Moranes, Curtisses, Blochs and Hurricanes [sic]. We were just able to watch the Do 17s before the dance began. There were three or four cockades for each one of us. Leutnant Fleitz had a scrap with a number of Moranes, one of which he shot down in flames. Then Leutnant Panthen and I became involved with six Hurricanes. Leutnant Panthen had one in front of him, but he turned away and I snapped up the bird. After a burst, during which I yelled "That's how it's done", he blew up. Panthen then chased another to a French forward airfield. He cracked up at the edge of the landing field and smouldered.

'Shortly before Paris another Morane climbed towards the bombers. I gained altitude and was able to approach the last one, which was lagging behind the others somewhat. The pilot probably had no idea that his end was near. I fired from 30 m, the crate being as big as a barn door in front of me. Its tail gone, wings in tatters, it went down and crashed into a block of houses.

'My *Staffel* had six victories but Leutnant Fleitz was missing. He had been shot down by a Morane and bailed out, only to be shot at from the ground [and killed] while hanging beneath his parachute.'

By now the Germans were advancing ever closer to Paris and claims for enemy aircraft soon began to reduce for I. *Gruppe*, with just five victories in June. The only loss was Unteroffizier Paul Grond, who was captured four days after he became lost during a transfer flight on 6 June. He returned on 6 July. Unusually, Grond was killed on 22 August 1944 while still with 1./JG 53 but with the rank of gefreiter. The same pace of activity was experienced by II. *Gruppe* (eight kills, and Oberleutnant Otto Böhner of *Stab*. II./JG 53 captured on 9 June). On 5 June I. *Gruppe* moved to Charleville (its last kill was on 9 June), then to Vraux and finally Rennes, in Brittany, while II. *Gruppe* moved to Charleville on 1 June (its last kill was claimed eight days later), then to Vraux and finally Dinan, also in Brittany.

It was a different matter for III. *Gruppe*, which operated from La Selve and Tours-sur-Marne during June, and claimed an astounding 50 victories between the 1st and 11th of that same month. During this period it suffered just three casualties in return, with Feldwebel Heinz Galubinski of 7./JG 53 being shot down and captured on 6 June (he claimed his ninth success that same day) and Feldwebel Hermann Veith of 8./JG 53 being killed 24 hours later (he had just one victory to his name). The first loss

Hauptmann Werner Mölders proudly wears the *Ritterkreuz* awarded to him for becoming the first German fighter pilot to achieve 20 victories in World War 2. Mölders' victories are well documented, so it remains a mystery as to why there are only 18 marked on the tailfin of his machine seen here. One suggestion is that this is Mölders' reserve Bf 109E which did not yet display the two victories he achieved northwest of Amiens on 27 May 1940 (*John Weal*)

endured by III. *Gruppe* had in fact occurred on 5 June – the very day Operation *Red* was launched – and it involved the Luftwaffe's leading ace at that time.

During the first three days of June Mölders' score had risen to 23. At 1020 hrs on the 5th he took off from La Selve to patrol in the Beauvais-Compiègne-Laon area, duly claiming a Bloch and a Potez 63 destroyed. After landing at 1200 hrs he took off again at 1730 hrs on a 'Freie Jagd' over Compiègne. His log book entry for this sortie read as follows;

'Hauptmann Mölders failed to return from an operational flight. 11 June 1940, the aircraft of Hauptmann Mölders was found in a wood east of Compiègne.'

In his biography Mölders describes what happened to him on 5 June;

'Aircraft above us. We cannot identify them. We climb to 7000 m but they are 109s [of I./JG 27] so we go down a little and get ready to fly home, but suddenly we see six Moranes. I prepare to attack, but right in the middle of my attack I see two unknown *Staffeln* of 109s which are attacking the same aircraft from behind and above. I watch this fight for a while, then I attack a Morane at which three 109s are firing, but all the time in vain as he is in a turn. I get him for a moment in my sights but he then breaks immediately. He suddenly climbs again below me – I lose sight of him under my wings – and then he comes again from the side, lower, and, what's more, he is firing but at an extreme range.

'I break briefly then climb towards the sun. He has probably lost me, as he turns in the opposite direction and heads south. Below, two 109s are still attacking a single Morane. I watch this fight, which goes down to hedge-hopping level, the Morane preventing effective shooting by continual turns. I glance behind and upwards to see 109s still wheeling about everywhere.

'I am flying at a height of 800 m when suddenly there are explosions and sparks in my cockpit. I am totally stunned. The throttle is destroyed and the control column jumps forward and I am in a vertical dive. I grasp the cockpit [canopy] jettison lever and the hood flies away. My aircraft levels out one last time, giving me the chance to undo my straps and raise myself in my seat. I am then free and the parachute has already opened. I see my aeroplane falling out of control, its port wing breaking up. Just before it hits the ground it pulls up, then it crashes vertically.

'Hanging on the parachute, I look round for my adversary but can only see 109s, which are circling me. I am silently floating towards the ground, which is still being held by the enemy as I am 60 km behind the frontline, west of Compiègne. I draw my pistol and, having cocked it, put it into my trouser pocket. The ground is coming up fast, so I bend my knees slightly and the impact is relatively soft. I immediately free myself from the parachute and run towards a wood. Frenchmen are running towards me from all sides, and as I reach the edge of the wood a bullet flies past my ears. I throw away my fur-lined flying jacket and run to the other end of the wood. A large field of lupins lies in front of me, so I crawl into it.'

The battle that had just taken place involved I./JG 27 as well as III./JG 53, the former unit claiming seven MS.406s and the latter two. GC II/7 reported losing five Dewoitine D.520s between Compiègne and Estreés-St-Denis, with three pilots wounded and two killed. One of those to die was six-victory ace Sous-Lt René Pomier Layrargues, who was almost certainly shot down by fellow ace Oberleutnant Gerhard Homuth, *Staffelkapitän* of 3./JG 27, just after the French pilot had apparently accounted for Mölders. Layrargues' D.520 crashed and burned at Marissel, on the outskirts of Beauvais, and his demise matches Homuth's seventh victory claim of the war.

Mölders' Bf 109E-4 crashed and exploded on the edge of a wood at Ferme du Villersau at Canly. He descended between Blincourt and Sacy-le-Petit and managed to evade capture for about an hour before being trapped by French soldiers. As a French officer quickly confiscated Mölders' *Ritterkreuz*, they must have realised they had captured someone important and, on the verge of being beaten, he managed to get into a car and was driven away.

Temporary command of III. *Gruppe* now went to Hauptmann Rolf Pingel. During the course of the next 48 hours III./JG 53 was credited with a further ten French fighters destroyed south of the Aisne. These were to be the *Geschwader*'s final successes of the *Blitzkrieg* in the west, for the remaining fortnight of the campaign saw little activity for the pilots of JG 53. On 20 June III. *Gruppe* was tasked with providing a fighter umbrella above the forest of Compiègne, where German and French representatives were beginning negotiations for an armistice. On the day the armistice was signed, 22 June, JG 53's units received orders to vacate the fields they had been occupying along the River Marne east of Paris and transfer westwards into Brittany. Here, based at Rennes (*Stab.* I. and III. *Gruppen*) and Dinan (II. *Gruppe*), JG 53 was to be responsible for guarding the coastline of northwestern France.

With the ceasefire in France coming into effect at 0035 hrs on 25 June, it was clear that the next stage of the hostilities would involve taking the war across the Channel to Great Britain. It was equally obvious that any such undertaking would be concentrated along the narrowest stretch of the Channel opposite southeast England. Having been only peripherally involved on the extreme left-hand flank of operations during much of the recent fighting in France, it appeared that the 'Ace of Spades' – now ordered to defend the westernmost and widest sector of the English Channel where it opened out on to the Atlantic Ocean – was again about to be sidelined in the forthcoming Battle of Britain.

25 June also saw Mölders released, as were the other JG 53 PoWs, namely Oberleutnant Wolf-Dietrich Wilcke and Oberfeldwebel Hans Galubinski, the latter having been mistreated when first captured.

The Battle of France now over, there was a brief respite before the Battle of Britain began, giving a chance for rest and

The Bf 109E featured in the previous photograph is now seen with a 19th victory bar on the fin. This is difficult to explain, because Mölders' tally jumped from 18 to 20 victories on 27 May when he claimed two 'Curtiss' fighters 15 km southwest of Amiens

Pilots of 7. *Staffel* come together for a group photograph immediately after the Battle of France had come to an end. They are, from left to right, Unteroffizier Hermann Neuhoff (40 victories, PoW from 10 April 1942), Feldwebel Hans Galubinski (28 victories, killed on 13 January 1944), Unteroffizier Hans-Georg Schulte (eight victories, PoW from 6 September 1940), Feldwebel Herbert Schramm (42 victories, killed on 1 December 1943), *Staffelkapitän* Oberleutnant Wolf-Dietrich Wilcke (155 victories, killed on 23 March 1944), Leutnant Hans Riegel (one victory, killed on 6 September 1940), Unteroffizier Ernst Poschenreider (PoW from 30 September 1940), Unteroffizier Adolf Kalkum (19 victories, survived) and Oberfeldwebel Franz Götz (63 victories, survived) (*Traebing*)

JG 53's top scorers from 1 January to 1 July 1940

NAME	STAFFEL/GRUPPE	VICTORIES
Hauptmann Werner Mölders	*Stab*. III	25
Oberleutnant Heinz Bretnütz	6.	9
Oberleutnant Hans-Karl Mayer	1.	9
Oberfeldwebel Hans Galubinski	7.	9
Oberleutnant Wolfgang Lippert	3.	8
Leutnant Freidrich-Karl Müller	8.	8
Unteroffizier Hermann Neuhoff	7.	8
Hauptmann Rolf Pingel	2. and *Stab*. III	8
Leutnant Heinz Kunert	9.	7
Oberleutnant Georg Claus	*Stab*. III	6
Oberleutnant Hans von Hahn	8	6
Oberleutnant Franz Götz	9.	5

recuperation and the posting in of replacement pilots. A number of experienced aviators were also posted to other units.

During the Battle of France *Stab*./JG 53 had claimed five victories without loss, I. *Gruppe* in the region of 64 victories for two killed, two captured and seven wounded, II. *Gruppe* had claimed about 30 victories for three pilots killed, one captured and two wounded and, finally, III. *Gruppe* was credited with about 98 victories, with three pilots killed and three captured.

A number of aces were now emerging, especially Mölders. However, he did not return to JG 53 after being released, instead being promoted to major and given command of JG 51 at the end of July 1940. His place as *Gruppenkommandeur* went to Hauptmann Harro Harder, who did not arrive until mid-July 1940. Although Harder had claimed 11 victories in the Spanish Civil War, he had added just one success (a PZL P.11 fighter over Poland on 9 September 1939) to his tally whilst serving as *Staffelkapitän* of 1.(*Jagd*)/*Lehrgeschwader* 2, after which he was posted away to be an instructor with *Jagdfliegerschule* 1 in October 1939.

The number of pilots who had five or more victories during the Battle of France would increase significantly during the second half of 1940, and some of these men were awarded the *Ritterkreuz*. However, three of them would not live to see 1941.

Both aces from the Spanish Civil War, Hauptleute Rolf-Peter Pingel (left) and Hans-Karl Mayer, the *Kapitäne* of 2. and 1. *Staffeln* respectively, enjoy a cigarette shortly after the fighting had ceased in France. Pingel had been credited with six victories between 14 May and 11 June 1940, while Mayer had gone one better during the same period. Both men had earlier claimed two successes during the 'Phoney War' and six each in Spain. Although Mayer would remain with I./JG 53 until his death in combat on 17 October 1940, Pingel transferred to I./JG 26 as its *Gruppenkommandeur* on 21 August 1940

CHAPTER THREE

BATTLE OF BRITAIN – THE WESTERN BATTLE

T he opening phase of the Battle of Britain only served to underline JG 53's isolation from the main scene of operations. The Luftwaffe's first objective was to deny the English Channel to British shipping. This was far more likely to be achieved along the narrower eastern end of the Channel, and in the 21-mile width of the Straits of Dover, than across the almost 100 miles of open water separating Brittany from the coasts of Devon and Cornwall.

Having been rushed up into Brittany even before the fighting in France had officially ceased, the *Geschwader*'s 120 'Emils' then spent the last week of June and all of July fruitlessly guarding this northwestern corner of the newly conquered country against raids that never materialised.

I./JG 53 was the first to arrive in Brittany, flying in to Rennes on 23 June. Two days later its pilots began making local flights to gain familiarity with the area over which they would be flying in the weeks to come. Meanwhile, the other two *Gruppen*, which had settled in at Dinan (II./JG 53) and Rennes (*Stab.* and III./JG 53), began to do the same. This quiet period also ushered in a number of changes of Executive Officers. Hauptmann Lothar von Janson handed over I. *Gruppe* to Major Albert

This photograph just predates the controversial replacement of the 'Pik-As' badge with a red band. This 1. *Staffel* aircraft, 'White 12', was assigned to Unteroffizier Willi Ghesla (centre), who was eventually shot down by Hurricanes and captured on 5 October 1940. Unteroffizier Werner Karl (who was also downed by Hurricanes, on 2 September 1940, and made a PoW) is standing on the left and future six-victory ace Unteroffizier Heinrich Höhnisch on the right. The latter was also shot down, on 9 September 1940, almost certainly falling victim to a No 19 Sqn Spitfire. Badly burned, Höhnisch bailed out near Biggin Hill and was captured upon landing

Oberleutnant Hans-Karl Mayer and Leutnant Alfred Zeis of 1. *Staffel* were photographed in front of the Trocadero in Paris during leave in late June 1940, prior to joining the rest of JG 53 in its move west. Although Zeis had claimed just a solitary victory (a 'Hawk 36' on 3 June) during the Battle of France, he would be credited with three more during August whilst flying from Cherbourg-East and the all-important fifth success on 12 September (a Blenheim off Le Havre). Zeis was shot down – probably by a No 1 Sqn (RCAF) Hurricane – on 5 October, bailing out over Pluckley, in Kent, and being taken prisoner upon landing

Blumensaat and was posted to the RLM. A number of staff and training appointments followed for von Janson until he was given command of *Zerstörergeschwader* (ZG) 1 in October 1943. He was shot down and reported missing over the Bay of Biscay on 10 March 1944.

With Harder's arrival in mid-July as the new *Gruppenkommandeur* of III./JG 53, Hauptmann Rolf Pingel was free to reassume command of 2. *Staffel*. Other changes were made at this time in III. *Gruppe*, with the newly released Oberleutnant Wolf-Dietrich 'Fürst' Wilcke resuming command of 7. *Staffel*, while Oberleutnant Ernst Boenigk was replaced by the more successful Oberleutnant Jakob Stoll as *Staffelkapitän* of 9./JG 53. Meanwhile, in II. *Gruppe*, Oberleutnant Hubert Kroeck took over JG 53's *Ergänzungsstaffel* (Operational Fighter Training Squadron), his place being taken by the more successful and popular Oberleutnant Günther Schulze-Blanck – other command changes would occur in II. *Gruppe* as the Battle of Britain progressed.

During this time, for reasons that are no longer entirely clear, the 'Pik-As' badge was ordered to be removed from the cowlings (and in some cases the tail swastika was also overpainted), to be replaced by a red band around the whole of the cowling. This might have been connected with the *Geschwaderkommodore* Oberstleutnant Hans-Jürgen von Cramon-Taubadel, who apparently was not popular with the Luftwaffe hierarchy. The official reason given for the adoption of this marking, which dated back to an order issued in late July, stated that it was an intelligence subterfuge. The 'Ace of Spades' had become too well known to the RAF, and the sudden appearance of the 'red stripe' unit was to fool the enemy into believing that an entirely new *Jagdgeschwader* had been added to the Luftwaffe's Channel front order of battle.

However, according to most people assigned to the unit at the time, the change was introduced not out of operational necessity, but as a result of personal antagonism. It was no secret that by this time Oberstleutnant von Cramon-Taubadel had become very much *persona non grata* within the Luftwaffe hierarchy – not least because he had chosen to marry a lady who was, in his own words, 'not wholly Aryan'. The red band was thus regarded as a snub to his command of the 'Ace of Spades'. If this was indeed the case, it was not the only injustice suffered by von Cramon, who, despite the successes of his *Geschwader* in France, had claimed only a single victory (an MS.406 on 21 December 1939) while he was leading I./JG 54.

Unlike many of his World War 1 contemporaries who commanded *Jagd-* and *Zerstörergeschwader* in 1940 – the likes of Harry von Bülow-Bothkamp, Joachim-Friedrich Huth, Max Ibel and Theo Osterkamp – von Cramon-Taubadel was never awarded the Knight's Cross. Indeed, he only received the *Deutsches Kreuz* in Gold towards the end of the conflict, having been promoted only to the rank of oberst. Von Cramon-Taubadel was destined to remain under something of a cloud for the rest of his Luftwaffe career, being shunted off to the backwaters of Scandinavia to serve as chief-of-staff to various local commands during the later years of the war. Perhaps not entirely by chance, it was not until after von Cramon-Taubadel had relinquished command of JG 53 *(text continues on page 41)*

34

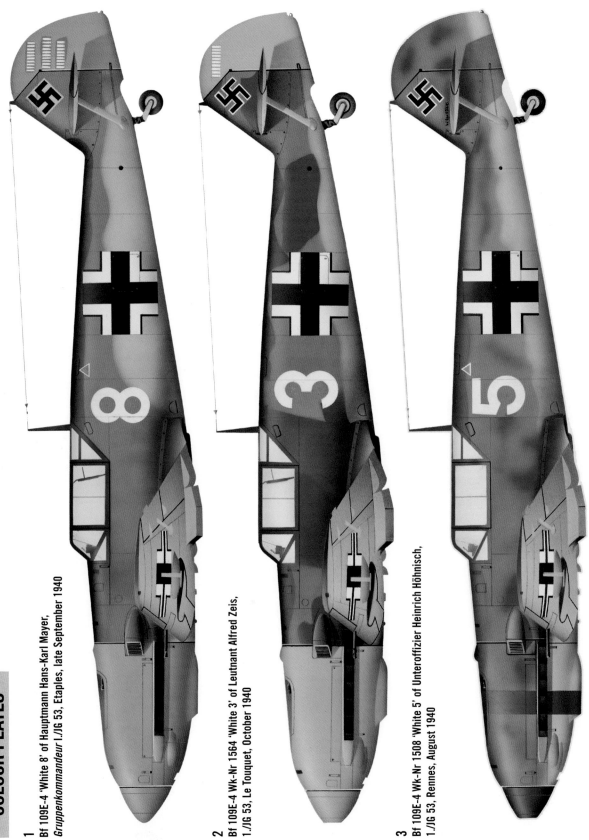

COLOUR PLATES

1
Bf 109E-4 'White 8' of Hauptmann Hans-Karl Mayer,
Gruppenkommandeur I./JG 53, Etaples, late September 1940

2
Bf 109E-4 Wk-Nr 1564 'White 3' of Leutnant Alfred Zeis,
1./JG 53, Le Touquet, October 1940

3
Bf 109E-4 Wk-Nr 1508 'White 5' of Unteroffizier Heinrich Höhnisch,
1./JG 53, Rennes, August 1940

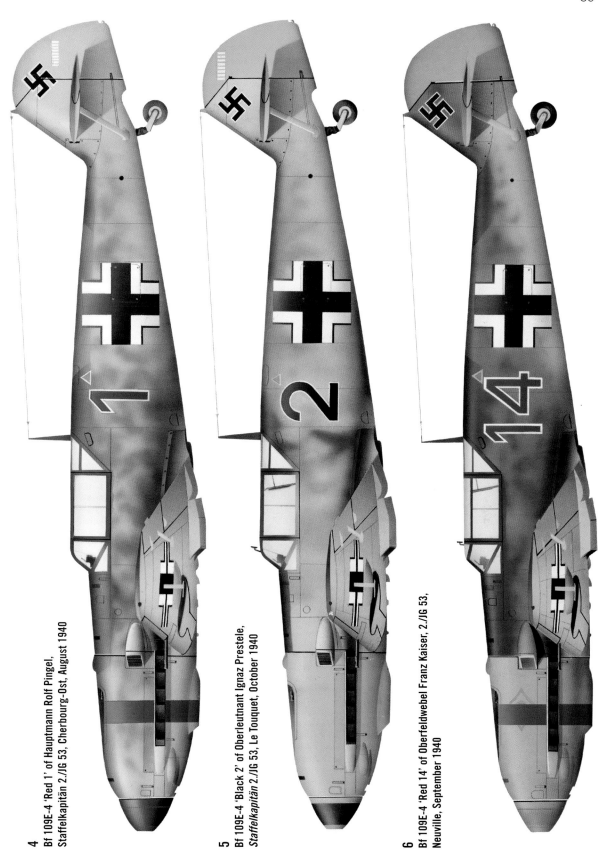

4
Bf 109E-4 'Red 1' of Hauptmann Rolf Pingel,
Staffelkapitän 2./JG 53, Cherbourg-Ost, August 1940

5
Bf 109E-4 'Black 2' of Oberleutnant Ignaz Prestele,
Staffelkapitän 2./JG 53, Le Touquet, October 1940

6
Bf 109E-4 'Red 14' of Oberfeldwebel Franz Kaiser, 2./JG 53,
Neuville, September 1940

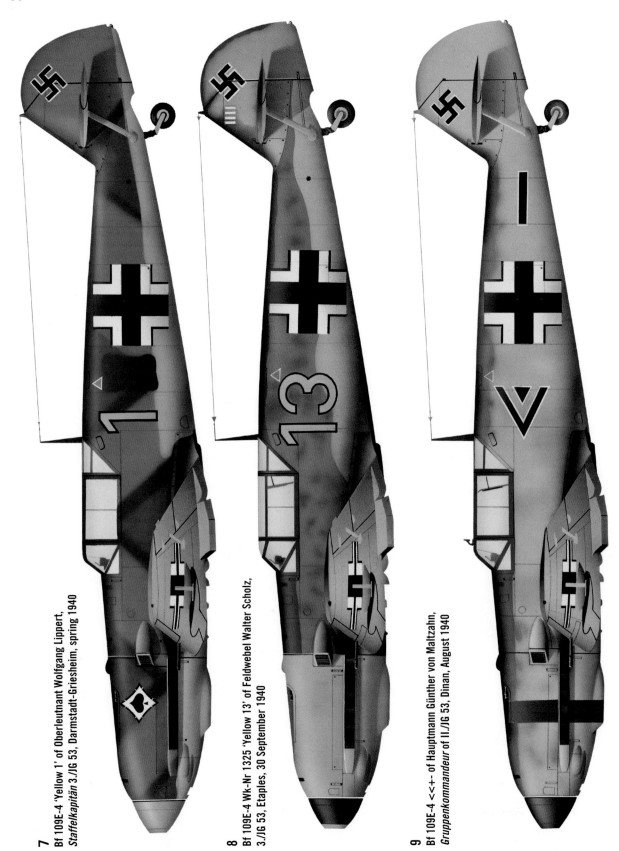

7
Bf 109E-4 'Yellow 1' of Oberleutnant Wolfgang Lippert,
Staffelkapitän 3./JG 53, Darmstadt-Griesheim, spring 1940

8
Bf 109E-4 Wk-Nr 1325 'Yellow 13' of Feldwebel Walter Scholz,
3./JG 53, Etaples, 30 September 1940

9
Bf 109E-4 <<+- of Hauptmann Günther von Maltzahn,
Gruppenkommandeur of II./JG 53, Dinan, August 1940

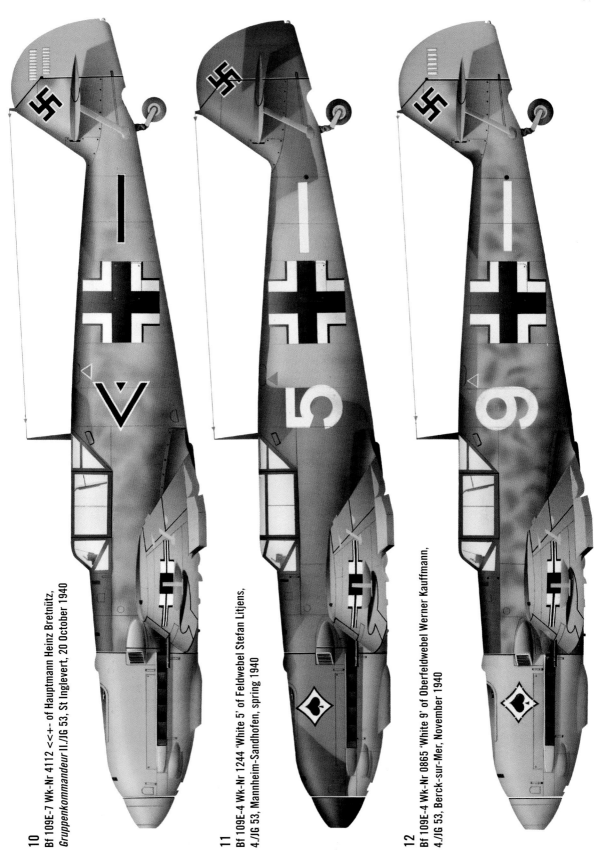

37

10
Bf 109E-7 Wk-Nr 4112 <<+- of Hauptmann Heinz Bretnütz,
Gruppenkommandeur II./JG 53, St Inglevert, 20 October 1940

11
Bf 109E-4 Wk-Nr 1244 'White 5' of Feldwebel Stefan Litjens,
4./JG 53, Mannheim-Sandhofen, spring 1940

12
Bf 109E-4 Wk-Nr 0865 'White 9' of Oberfeldwebel Werner Kauffmann,
4./JG 53, Berck-sur-Mer, November 1940

38

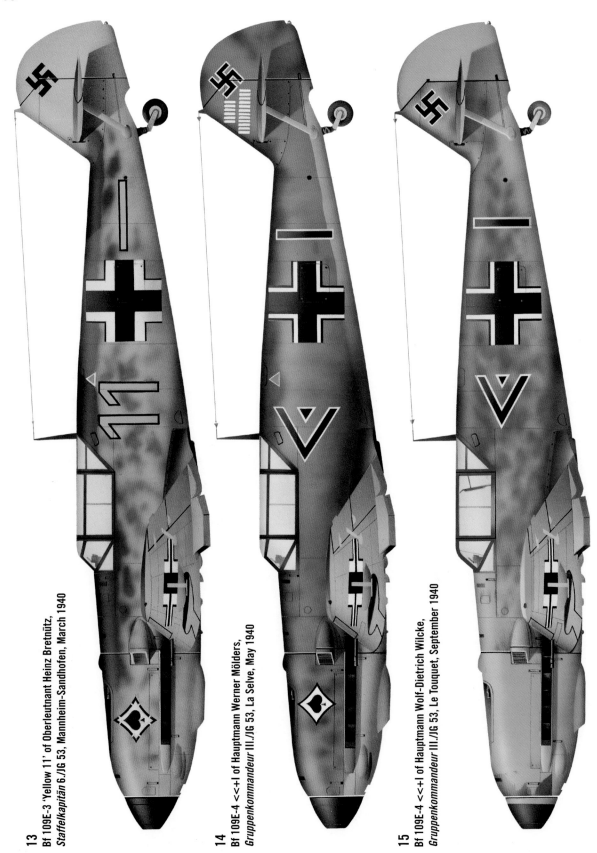

13
Bf 109E-3 'Yellow 11' of Oberleutnant Heinz Bretnütz,
Staffelkapitän 6./JG 53, Mannheim-Sandhofen, March 1940

14
Bf 109E-4 <<+l of Hauptmann Werner Mölders,
Gruppenkommandeur III./JG 53, La Selve, May 1940

15
Bf 109E-4 <<+l of Hauptmann Wolf-Dietrich Wilcke,
Gruppenkommandeur III./JG 53, Le Touquet, September 1940

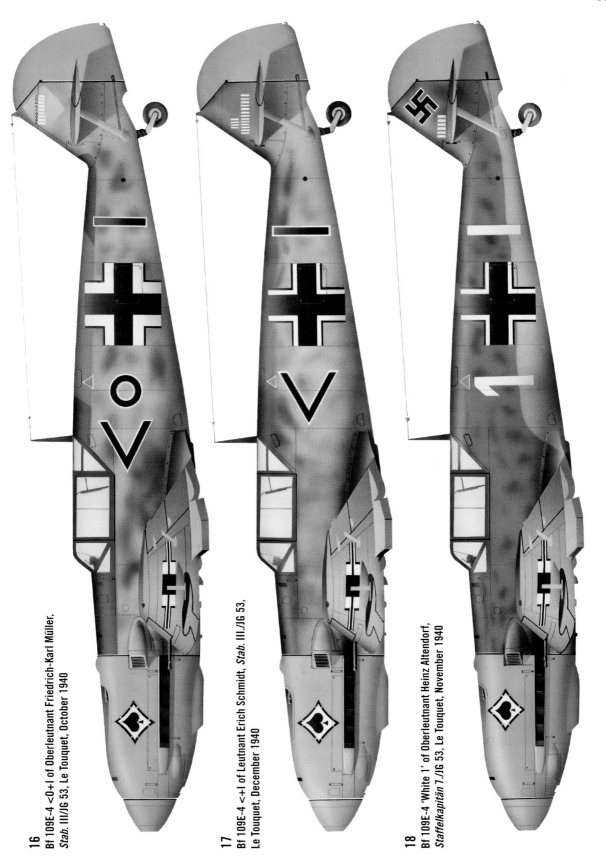

16
Bf 109E-4 <0+I of Oberleutnant Friedrich-Karl Müller,
Stab. III./JG 53, Le Touquet, October 1940

17
Bf 109E-4 <+I of Leutnant Erich Schmidt, *Stab.* III./JG 53,
Le Touquet, December 1940

18
Bf 109E-4 'White 1' of Oberleutnant Heinz Altendorf,
Staffelkapitän 7./JG 53, Le Touquet, November 1940

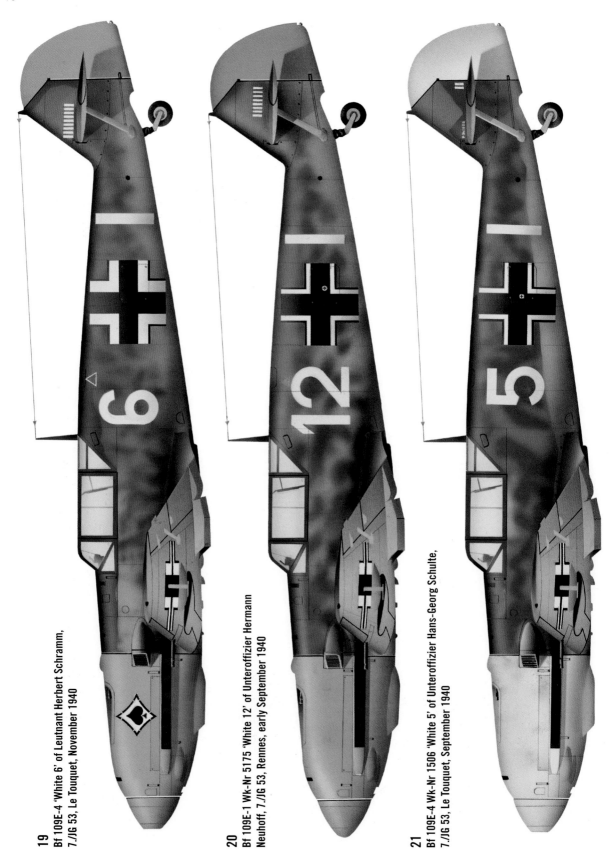

19
Bf 109E-4 'White 6' of Leutnant Herbert Schramm,
7./JG 53, Le Touquet, November 1940

20
Bf 109E-1 Wk-Nr 5175 'White 12' of Unteroffizier Hermann
Neuhoff, 7./JG 53, Rennes, early September 1940

21
Bf 109E-4 Wk-Nr 1506 'White 5' of Unteroffizier Hans-Georg Schulte,
7./JG 53, Le Touquet, September 1940

Future 68-victory ace Leutnant Gerhard Michalski, *Gruppen*Adjutant of II./JG 53, poses alongside Hauptmann Günther von Maltzahn's Bf 109E-4 at Dinan, south of Saint-Malo, in early August 1940. This aeroplane was one of the first to have the 'red band', which completely encircled the engine cowling, applied in place of the 'Pik-As' emblem. The edict ordering the application of this marking was issued in late July. Michalski would claim his first success on 15 August 1940 whilst flying from Dinan, and he had six victories to his name by 30 November that same year. The *Gruppen*Adjutant of II./JG 53, he is pictured in front of the machine flown by his *Kommandeur*, Hauptmann Günther von Maltzahn. The freshly applied unit marking, completely encircling the engine cowling, is clearly visible

Most of JG 53's early operations over the western Channel during the first weeks of the Battle of Britain were staged out of either Cherbourg or the Channel Islands. At Villiaze, on Guernsey, its *Emils* were refuelled with the aid of one of Mr Miller's Commer Trucks (the vehicle has presumably not been officially requisitioned as it still bears its civilian number plate) (*John Weal*)

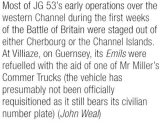
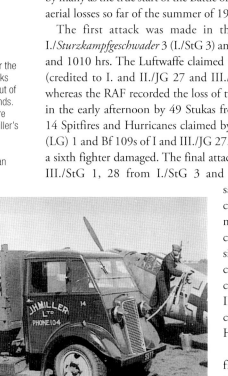

(some considerable time thereafter, in fact – the powers-that-be did not want to make the connection too obvious) that the 'Ace of Spades' was reinstated on the *Geschwader*'s fighters.

July and the first week of August 1940 were uneventful for the whole *Geschwader*, with just the occasional *Alarmstart* (scramble) and cancelled escort missions due to poor weather. A few accidents occurred (four in total to 9 August), but at last, on 8 August, the first victories were achieved. The target that day, first by E-Boats off Newhaven and then three separate attacks by Stukas off the Isle of Wight, was westward-headed Convoy CW 9, codenamed *Peewit*. The targeting of this convoy is now regarded by many as the true start of the Battle of Britain, as this day saw the heaviest aerial losses so far of the summer of 1940.

The first attack was made in the morning by 29 Stukas from I./*Sturzkampfgeschwader* 3 (I./StG 3) and 28 from III./StG 1 between 1005 and 1010 hrs. The Luftwaffe claimed three Spitfires and two Hurricanes (credited to I. and II./JG 27 and III./StG 1) for the loss of one Stuka, whereas the RAF recorded the loss of two Hurricanes. The second attack, in the early afternoon by 49 Stukas from I. and III./StG 2, saw another 14 Spitfires and Hurricanes claimed by the Bf 110s of V./*Lehrgeschwader* (LG) 1 and Bf 109s of I and III./JG 27. The RAF lost five aircraft and had a sixth fighter damaged. The final attack that evening, by 22 Stukas from III./StG 1, 28 from I./StG 3 and 32 from *Stab*. and II./StG 77, saw 17 Spitfires and Hurricanes confirmed as destroyed and three more as probables. RAF records confirm the loss of six aircraft, with six more damaged. Luftwaffe records confirm that in addition to the claims by V./LG 1, II. and III./JG 27 and ZG 2, II./JG 53 claimed two Spitfires and a Hurricane without loss.

Both I. and II./JG 53 operated from Guernsey that afternoon, I. *Gruppe* being recalled without incident, thus leaving the first victories to be claimed by Hauptmann Günther von Maltzahn (*Gruppenkommandeur* of II. *Gruppe*), Oberleutnant Richard Vogel (4. *Staffel*) and Hauptmann Heinz Bretnütz (*Staffelkapitän* of 6. *Staffel*) – these were the third victories for the first two pilots and the tenth for Bretnütz. However, it was clear that the Luftwaffe was wildly optimistic with its claims, so it is hard to ascertain who got whom.

Owing to poor weather over the Channel, 9 and 10 August saw no meaningful activity, but that changed the following day. The target was Portland harbour, which was attacked by 38 Junkers Ju 88s from I. and II./Kampfgeschwader (KG) 54, supported by two Heinkel He 111s for air-sea rescue purposes.

The escort for the bombers was massive, involving all three *Gruppen* of JG 2, JG 27 and JG 53 and the first two *Gruppen* of ZG 2. Again, claims were wildly inflated (57 RAF aircraft during the whole day, which was then amended to 59), but Leutnant Werner Heidrich of 2. *Staffel* was credited with two Spitfires and Oberleutnant Kurt Brändle (recently recovered from his injuries as a result of his accident on 26 May) of 4. *Staffel* claimed another. However, most of the victories went to III. *Gruppe*, its new *Gruppenkommandeur*, Hauptmann Harro Harder, claiming three Spitfires to take his score to four. Feldwebel Anton Ochsenkuhn and Unteroffizier Kurt Sauer of 9. *Staffel* each claimed a Spitfire.

All three *Gruppen* returned to France having suffered no losses, but from now on attrition would start to creep up, starting with 12 August, which saw the loss of one, and almost two, *Gruppenkommandeurs*.

During the late morning of the 12th 63 Ju 88s of KG 51 took off and headed for Portsmouth harbour and the radar station at Ventnor, on the Isle of Wight. The massive escort comprised Bf 110s of ZG 2 and ZG 76 and Bf 109s from JG 2, JG 27 and JG 53. The Luftwaffe report of the attack, filed at 0115 hrs the following morning, states that 36 RAF fighters were confirmed shot down and another seven probably shot down for the loss of 11 Ju 88s, five Bf 110s and a single Bf 109, further naming the loss of Oberst Fisser from KG 51 and Hauptmann Harder from III./JG 53.

The best account of what happened to JG 53 on 12 August comes from reports filed by 1./JG 53, the only *Staffel* from I. *Gruppe* to achieve victories, claiming four Hurricanes. Amongst the successful pilots was recently promoted Hauptmann Hans-Karl Mayer, who submitted the following combat report;

'Mission – Fighter sweep into the area around the Isle of Wight–Portsmouth. I was leading the *Staffel* at 8500 m when [at 1220 hrs] far below I saw three aircraft hanging around the scene of a crash in the water. I descended immediately, and over the sight of another crash found a flight of three Hurricanes attacking a damaged Bf 110. Before I could attack, the Bf 110 burst into flames on its right side. The pilot bailed out. I attacked the aircraft on the right of the formation and set it on fire; it subsequently dove vertically into the sea. My wingman [Unteroffizier Heinrich Rühl] shot down the left aircraft. The English flight leader

Hauptmann Hans-Karl Mayer poses cheerfully on the tail of his Bf 109E-4 'White 8', which displays a gaping hole next to the aircraft jacking point. The fighter had been badly damaged in combat with three Hurricanes (probably from No 145 Sqn) off the Isle of Wight on 12 August 1940. Mayer was credited with two Hurricanes destroyed on this date

Very few photographs of Hauptmann Harro Harder, briefly *Gruppenkommandeur* of III./JG 53, exist. He is seen here, far left, on his arrival, on or about 13 July 1940. Closest to the camera is Oberleutnant Jakob Stoll, who assumed command of 9. *Staffel* from Oberleutnant Ernst Boenigk, to his right. Harder, who had claimed 11 victories in Spain, downed a PZL 'P.24' (almost certainly a P.11) over Poland on 9 September 1939 whilst serving with 1.(J)/LG 2 and two Spitfires and three Hurricanes (two of the latter remained unconfirmed) with III./JG 53 prior to being lost in action on 12 August 1940. Stoll had been credited with 13 victories (and a 14th unconfirmed) by the time he was killed in action on 17 September 1940

subsequently fought with other machines of the *Staffel* until I was able to shoot him down.'

It is possible that Mayer and Rühl shot down Plt Off John Harrison and Acting Flt Lt Wilhelm Pankratz and Sgt Josef Kwiecinski, all of No 145 Sqn, who were reported missing off the Isle of Wight while defending against the attack on Portsmouth. These victories were the tenth and eleventh for Mayer and the first for Heinrich Rühl and Unteroffizier Heinrich Kopperschläger. Although II. *Gruppe* filed no claims, III. *Gruppe* was credited with two, one of which went to Leutnant Erich Schmidt of 9. *Staffel* – by the end of 1940 he had a further 16 victories to his name. Two more claims were unconfirmed.

Hauptmann Harro Harder reported over the radio that he had shot down two Hurricanes at 1320 hrs and 1325 hrs (almost an hour after Schmidt's claim), and he was last seen at 1335 hrs. On 19 September the body of the 27-year-old fighter pilot – one of just 28 who had been awarded the Spanish Cross in Gold with Swords and Diamonds – was washed ashore at Dieppe. He is now buried in the military war cemetery at Champigny-St-André. In the same combat, another recipient of the Spanish Cross in Gold with Swords and Diamonds, Hauptmann Max Graf Hoyos (*Staffelkapitän* of 8./ZG 76) was shot down too. His body was also washed ashore in France, and he is buried in the same military cemetery as Harder. Although, officially, Harder had four confirmed victories, he has been included in this volume as a 'Pik-As' ace because his two unconfirmed successes from his last flight have been included in his tally.

What happened to Harder remains a mystery. It has been suggested that he was shot down by either Plt Off David Crook of No 609 Sqn or Plt Off James Strickland of No 213 Sqn (both pilots would end the Battle of Britain as aces), but between the two units, the RAF claimed the destruction of six Bf 109s when only one, Harder's, was lost.

Command of III. *Gruppe* now passed temporarily to Hauptmann Wolf-Dietrich Wilcke, with his 7. *Staffel* being led by Oberleutnant Hans

A pre-war pilot with 1./JG 53, Leutnant Georg Claus became *Technischer Offizier* of III./JG 53 in November 1939. Seen here during the winter of 1939-40, Claus had been credited with six victories (and two more unconfirmed) by the time he transferred to JG 51 at the end of August 1940. He was killed in action on 11 November that year while commanding 1./JG 51, his score then standing at 11 (with seven unconfirmed)

This photograph of Oberleutnant Georg Claus was taken shortly after he had left *Stab*. III./JG 53 for JG 51, having joined the latter unit follow a request by his old commanding officer, Major Werner Mölders. Claus claimed his last victory with JG 53 on 15 August (*Rene Wouters*)

Riegel. However, it appears that being *Gruppenkommandeur* of III./JG 53 was a dangerous job, as while Wilcke was searching for Hauptmann Harder that afternoon his Bf 109 suffered engine failure and he was obliged to bail out over the Channel. Wilcke was finally picked up by a Dornier Do 18 flying boat that night thanks to Oberleutnant Georg 'Schorse' Claus from *Stab*. III./JG 53, who had gone along on the air-sea rescue mission to look for his *Gruppenkommandeur*. Wilcke was recovered apparently none the worse for wear and was soon permanently confirmed as *Gruppenkommandeur*, but he had to wait until the end of the month to get his next victory, his fourth of the war.

The following day (13 August) was designated *Alder Tag* (Eagle Day) by the Germans, but weather again hampered operations. After an uneventful mission in the morning, with just II. *Gruppe* claiming a Blenheim and a Hurricane, JG 53 was involved escorting Ju 88s and Stukas to attack Portland harbour and Andover and Middle Wallop airfields. The Portland attack was cancelled owing to poor weather, but this did not stop the escorting fighter pilots from claiming 35 RAF aircraft throughout the day – JG 53 was credited with four Hurricanes, four Spitfires and two Blenheims. Of note was the 'Freie Jagd' flown by I. *Gruppe*, which saw Hans-Karl Mayer increase his score to 12, while Unteroffizier Heinrich Höhnisch claimed two Hurricanes to take his tally to six. However, Höhnisch almost became a victim himself, as he later recalled;

'On 13 August 1940 I was hit by machine gun fire in my starboard wing by a Hurricane which came up behind me. I was forced by him to roll and dive away, but he chased me at sea level all the way back to Cherbourg, where he turned away.'

II. *Gruppe* claimed four Spitfires and a Hurricane, with future aces Oberleutnant Günther Schulze-Blanck and Feldwebel Stefan Litjens of 4. *Staffel* claiming their second and third victories, respectively. However, on the debit side, the *Gruppe* lost four aircraft in combat, with three pilots being captured and one killed. Furthermore, two aircraft were involved in takeoff accidents at Dinan.

Hauptmann Wolf-Dietrich Wilcke (right) was promoted to *Gruppenkommandeur* of III./JG 53 following the death of Hauptmann Harro Harder. He is seen here with Oberleutnant Jürgen Harder, the younger brother of Harro, who joined 7. *Staffel* in early 1941. Harder junior became a successful fighter pilot in his own right, claiming 56 victories with JG 53 and being awarded the *Ritterkreuz mit Eichenlaub*. He was killed in a flying accident on 17 February 1945 while commanding JG 11

The almost unrecognisable remains of the first JG 53 fighter to end up on mainland Britain is seen in Poole after being recovered from the town's harbour. This aircraft, Bf 109E-4 'Black 10' of 5. *Staffel*, was abandoned by a badly wounded Unteroffizier Willi Hohenfeldt after he was attacked at 18,000 ft by an RAF fighter while escorting bombers targeting the Dorset coast on 13 August 1940. II./JG 53 lost four Bf 109Es in combat that day (plus two in takeoff accidents at Dinan), with three pilots captured and one killed

For III. *Gruppe* there was just one claim that day, for a Blenheim by Unteroffizier Hans-Georg Schulte of 7. *Staffel*. However, there was just one Blenheim loss on the 13th – an aircraft of No 114 Sqn flown by Plt Off Illtyd Carson near Jersey – but there were two claims for a Blenheim destroyed by JG 53, as well as *Flakabteilung* 364 being credited with shooting down a Blenheim northeast of Cherbourg.

The next day of note in respect to action was 15 August, known afterwards as *Der Schwarzer Donnerstag* (Black Thursday). Over England that afternoon the only confirmed 'Pik-As' claims were by I./JG 53's Hauptmann Rolf Pingel (his ninth victory) and Hauptmann Hans-Karl Mayer, the latter's being a Hurricane 'near Salisbury'. This was probably Flg Off Gordon 'Mouse' Cleaver of No 601 Sqn, who bailed out wounded near Winchester. Mayer's combat report noted;

'I was leading the *Staffel* at 7000 m over a formation of bombers. Enemy fighters appeared as these began their diving attack. I descended at once and attacked a Hurricane that was on the tail of a Bf 110. When the enemy pilot spotted me he attempted to escape by diving. I closed in behind him and was able to get off three bursts. The enemy aircraft then dived absolutely vertically all the way to the ground.'

The last moments of a Hurricane reputed to have been shot down by JG 53. The unit encountered numerous examples of the RAF's staple fighter during 1939-40, this machine appearing to be trailing smoke as its pilot struggles to throw off his pursuer

Although I./JG 53 had only managed to down two aircraft, 1. *Staffel* did destroy six of the 16 barrage balloons claimed by the *Geschwader* that day, much to the alarm of the Winchester Royal Observer Corps, who thought the balloons were aircraft crashing in flames.

Meanwhile, off Portland, the only successes for II. *Gruppe* went to 6. *Staffel*, Hauptmann Heinz Bretnütz claiming two fighters to take his score to 12, Feldwebel Albrecht Baun scoring his fifth victory and Leutnant Gerhard Michalski his first of an eventual 68.

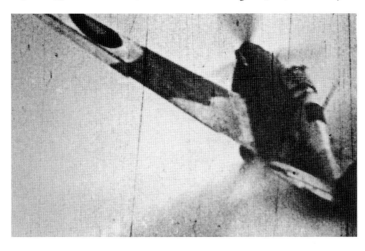

However, as the German aircraft headed back for France a number of RAF fighters followed them. Scrambled from Middle Wallop, No 234 Sqn was actively involved in the series of aerial battles that followed the Luftwaffe attacks, claiming four Bf 110s and three Bf 109s destroyed and fourth 'Emil' probably destroyed. These claims were optimistic, however, as Luftwaffe records show that only four Stukas, seven Ju 88s and six Bf 110s were lost in two attacks that evening. In addition to No 234 Sqn's victories, Fighter Command pilots claimed no fewer than ten Ju 88s, one Bf 109, 33 Bf 110s, eight Stukas and an He 111 destroyed, ten Ju 88s, one Bf 109 and one Do 215 probably destroyed and five Ju 88s, two Bf 110s and an He 111 damaged. However, German claims were not much better, with pilots stating that they had destroyed 54 RAF fighters.

Nevertheless, Luftwaffe records mention two RAF losses that cannot be disputed. An RAF pilot was picked up by German Air Sea Rescue and, unusually, a Spitfire landed at Théville (also known as Cherbourg-East), its pilot being taken prisoner. In fact No 234 Sqn lost three pilots that evening, two of whom were captured. It appears that Plt Off Vincent Parker (who was born in England and raised in Australia) strayed too close to the French coast while chasing a damaged Bf 110 of *Stab*. II./ZG 76 and fell victim to his intended prey. Unteroffizier Willy Lehner, radio operator/gunner to Leutnant Siegfried Hahn, reported shooting down a Spitfire off Cherbourg before Hahn crash-landed the damaged fighter at Cherbourg-West. Parker crashed in the sea off Cherbourg, where he was picked up by a German motor torpedo boat.

The other loss was that of Plt Off Richard Hardy, whose Spitfire had clearly been damaged in combat off Cherbourg. His return flight to

Spitfire I N3277 of No 234 Sqn is examined by curious groundcrew from JG 53 shortly after it landed at Cherbourg-East during the afternoon of 15 August 1940. Plt Off Richard Hardy was forced down at III./JG 53's airfield by Oberleutnant Georg Claus following combat over the Channel. The shell hole behind the cockpit was reportedly caused by German anti-aircraft guns, which opened fire when the Spitfire appeared over Cherbourg-East unannounced. However, according to eyewitness Oberleutnant Hans von Hahn, 'luckily the 20 mm flak failed to hit him'!

Middle Wallop was blocked by the returning German fighters, as Oberleutnant Hans von Hahn recalled;

'The other day [Oberleutnant Georg] Claus brought a Spitfire to Cherbourg. He caught it in the middle of the Channel, the Tommy making off to the south. Claus improved each of his turns with a brief burst of tracer fire. So it went all the way to Cherbourg airfield. There, the Tommy lowered his undercarriage and luckily the 20 mm flak failed to hit him. Then he landed safely and taxied in.'

On the ground, German airmen at Théville were shocked to see an enemy aircraft suddenly appear overhead unannounced, as one of them recalled;

'Somebody shouted "Spitfire!", and I looked up to see a Spitfire coming over the airfield. Flak opened fire and the Spitfire banked around and landed. Having got over the shock, we crowded around the Spitfire. The pilot got out and surrendered to Hauptmann Rolf Pingel.'

Future ace Leutnant Karl Leonhard was one of those to surround the aeroplane once it had come to a halt;

'The English pilot slid back the cockpit hood and immediately raised his hands – he obviously expected to be shot at once otherwise. He was just as surprised when I asked him to lower his hands and instead to climb out and come to the pilots' Mess to have a glass of champagne with the pilots of I./JG 53.'

Plt Off Richard Hardy was participating in No 234 Sqn's first action of the Battle of Britain, flying from Middle Wallop, on 15 August 1940 when his section was bounced by III./JG 53 off Swanage and four Spitfires were hit hard. Plt Off Cecil Hight was killed and Plt Offs Hardy and Vincent 'Bush' Parker were captured. The fourth Spitfire, flown by Sgt Zygmunt Klein, crash-landed near Twyford, in Hampshire

Hardy, who had suffered shrapnel wounds in the back probably from a cannon shell that had entered the fuselage immediately behind the cockpit on the port side, was quickly patched up and then entertained by the German pilots, before heading off to captivity. Credit for his capture went to Oberleutnant Georg Claus of Stab. III./JG 53, this being his seventh and last claim with JG 53, for at the end of the month he joined his old friend Major Werner Mölders at JG 51, becoming its Geschwader Adjutant in place of Oberleutnant Erich Kircheis, who had been shot down and taken prisoner on 28 August. Claus' first victories with his new unit came on the evening of that same day, and by the end of October 1940 he had moved to command 1. Staffel. He was reported missing over the Thames Estuary on 11 November, shot down flying a brand new Bf 109F-1, by which time his victory tally stood at 15.

For the Luftwaffe, 16 August began early with a weather aircraft taking off at 0440 hrs to look at the area southwest of London. This was followed by a second weather aeroplane an hour later, investigating the weather over western England. Four hours later, two Ju 88s took off to reconnoitre airfields in southern England, and this seems to have been the pattern for the morning – armed reconnaissance and weather reconnaissance missions, all without incident. However, just after midday, 104 Stuka dive-bombers took to the air and, together with their escort of 257 Bf 109s and 11 Bf 110s, headed towards the airfields of Tangmere, Lee-on-Solent and Gosport and Ventnor radar station. Eight RAF squadrons were scrambled to intercept and Nos 1, 43, 601 and 602 Sqns went after the Stukas off Selsey Bill while the remainder, including No 249 Sqn, engaged the escorts.

Two units, Hurricane-equipped No 249 Sqn flying from Boscombe Down and Spitfire-equipped No 152 Sqn based at Warmwell, had been told to patrol to the west of Southampton, and they were joined by Hurricanes of Nos 87 and 213 Sqns up from Exeter. Leading Red Section was A Flight Commander 23-year-old Londoner Flt Lt James Nicolson. The others in the Section were 29-year-old Sqn Ldr Eric 'Whizzy' King (who was gaining combat experience before taking command of No 151 Sqn) and 19-year-old Plt Off Martyn King, who had joined No 249 Sqn a little over two months before.

The squadron was aware of German fighters and, seeing three unidentified aircraft in the distance, Nicolson asked to investigate, and he and his Section broke away, only to be beaten to the contacts by No 152 Sqn. The three Hurricane pilots then turned to re-join the squadron, climbing from 15,000 ft to 17,500 ft and hearing 'Tally Ho' as their squadron went after more German aircraft. It was then that disaster struck, as Nicolson later recalled;

'Immediately after I was struck in the cockpit by four successive cannon shells, damaging the hood, setting fire to the reserve tank and wounding myself in the leg and thigh.'

Not only was Nicolson's Hurricane fatally hit, but so was Martyn King's, while 'Whizzy' King's aeroplane was damaged. None of the three RAF pilots saw their assailant/assailants, but Heinz Bretnütz, *Staffelkapitän* of 6./JG 53, claimed to have bounced two Hurricanes at 1336 hrs and 1337 hrs, shooting them down in quick succession. His two confirmed victories on 16 August were his 13th and 14th of the war. Due to the location, the time and his statement that he shot down two Hurricanes almost simultaneously, it is believed that Bretnütz was the pilot who bounced Red Section of No 249 Sqn.

Nicolson knew he had to get out of his burning aeroplane;

'I immediately pulled my feet up on to the seat and at the same time I put the nose down and dived steep, turning right. Saw Me 110 diving at same angle and converging – opened fire at approximately 200 yards and fired until I could bear heat no more.'

Although he assumed that he had been bounced by a Bf 110 that he then shot down, German records prove conclusively that no claims were filed by the sole Bf 110 unit flying that day, and none were lost. Unlike the previous day, Luftwaffe claims were surprisingly accurate in numbers, fighters and the Stukas claiming nine when the RAF lost seven fighters. The RAF in turn claimed 27 Stukas destroyed, six probables and eight damaged, as well as three Bf 109s destroyed. German losses were nine Stukas destroyed and eight damaged, while two Bf 109s collided off the Isle of Wight with the loss of one pilot. This time it was the RAF's turn to over-inflate its claims.

However, what Nicolson did showed incredible bravery, especially as, afterwards, he admitted to his squadron commander, 'My reflector sight was on but I cannot swear whether the firing button was at safe or fire.' Furthermore, he added, 'Eyewitnesses on the ground state that the Me 110 zig-zagged and dived steeply after Hurricane opened fire.' Nicolson managed to get away from his fighter with great difficulty, and after dropping 500 ft he opened his parachute. Had he looked around he would have possibly seen Martyn King, and the two of them now caused a tragic accident.

Hauptmann Heinz Bretnütz of 6./JG 53 was probably the pilot who shot down Flt Lt James Nicholson and Plt Off Martyn King of No 249 Sqn on 16 August 1940, these being the ace's 12th and 13th victories. His score had increased to 25 by year-end

Seeing two parachutes falling together, apparently a Royal Artillery officer told his men to take post and open fire in the belief that they were German parachutists. They were also joined by Home Guards, who then took pot-shots at the helpless RAF pilots. Martyn King was either mortally wounded in the bounce or his parachute collapsed due to damage from German cannon shell fragments, his body falling at Toothill, south of Romsey. James Nicolson, already suffering from burns to his face and hands, a severed eyelid and gunshot wounds to his leg and thigh, was now wounded in the buttocks as he floated down over the Millbrook region of Southampton. His Hurricane crashed at Rownhams School, while he landed in Burrowdale Road, Millbrook.

Meanwhile, No 249 Sqn, including Sqn Ldr 'Whizzy' King, returned without further incident. One of the unit's pilots recorded what had happened;

'[King] was excited. Garrulous. Hurrying about. His face creased by sweat and the lines of his oxygen mask. Yes, he'd been hit and damaged. No, he wasn't wounded but the others had gone. Both shot down. In flames. The blighters had come down and caught them unawares. Down from behind. He was in a highly emotional state and kept talking about tactics. We'd have to do things differently. Talking quickly and gesticulating.'

Six days later 'Whizzy' King took command of No 151 Sqn at North Weald, in Essex. On 24 August his Hurricane's propeller was shot off by a German fighter, but he managed to glide back to North Weald. Six days after that he was bounced over Maidstone and killed at the controls. His Hurricane smashed into the ground at Temple Street, Stroud, in Kent, taking him with it.

James Nicolson was rushed to Southampton and South Hants Hospital, where a few days later he was able to dictate what had happened to his Squadron Commander. After three weeks he was moved to the RAF hospital at Halton, and in November 1940 he went to Torquay to convalesce. It was there that he was notified of the following;

'The King has been graciously pleased to confer the Victoria Cross on Flt Lt James Brindley Nicolson of No 249 Sqn in recognition of most conspicuous bravery. During an engagement with the enemy near Southampton on 16 August 1940, Flt Lt Nicolson's aircraft was hit by four cannon shells, two of which wounded him whilst another set fire to the gravity tank. When about to abandon his aircraft owing to flames in the cockpit, he sighted an enemy fighter. This he attacked and shot down, although as a result of staying in his burning aircraft he sustained serious burns to his hands, face, neck and legs.'

There were other claims for JG 53 on 16 August, but not at the time that the Victoria Cross was being won. That evening, Hauptmann Wolfgang Lippert of 3. *Staffel* was credited with his ninth victory, a Spitfire, while II. *Gruppe's* Hauptmann Günther von Maltzahn (his fourth), Oberleutnant Kurt Brändle (his third) and Oberfeldwebel Werner Kauffmann (his fourth) of 4. *Staffel* were also successful. III. *Gruppe* reported no claims.

There were a number of losses too. Feldwebel Christian Hansen of 2. *Staffel* crash-landed on the Isle of Wight and was captured, and in II. *Gruppe* Gefreiter Karl Schulz of 6. *Staffel* ditched south of the Isle of Wight and was rescued unhurt (his second ditching, on 25 October,

Hauptmann Rolf Pingel (centre, facing the camera) transferred to I./JG 26 as its new *Gruppenkommandeur* on or about 22 August 1940. Seen here just prior to his departure, Pingel is talking to (right) Hauptmann Wolfgang Lippert, *Staffelkapitän* of 3./JG 53, who departed for II./JG 27 at the start of September, Oberleutnant Ignaz Prestele (far left), who replaced Pingel as *Staffelkapitän* of 2./JG 53, and, to Prestele's left, Leutnant Karl Leonhard of 3. *Staffel*, who survived the war

would result in his death). Feldwebel Fritz Dinger of 6. *Staffel* also ditched after being wounded, and he too was rescued. Finally, a Bf 109E-1 landed back at Guernsey with combat damage. Fritz Dinger was another 'Pik-As' pilot who was relatively unknown in 1940 but who later went on to do bigger and better things. His first success was apparently not until 4 July 1941 over the Soviet Union, but by the time of his death on 27 July 1943 in an air raid on Scalea, in Sicily, he had 64 victories to his name and had been awarded the *Deutsches Kreuz* in Gold and the *Ritterkreuz*.

Another day of rest for the Luftwaffe came on 17 August, in preparation for more heavy fighting on the 18th. However, on the latter date, JG 53 was not involved in any way until the afternoon, when it was tasked with escorting Stukas attacking the airfields at Thorney Island and Tangmere, in West Sussex. Just three claims were made, all for 2. *Staffel*, with one of them being the last for Hauptmann Rolf Pingel (his tenth), as he was posted to command I./JG 26 three days later. This transfer came about as a direct result of Reichsmarschall Hermann Göring enforcing the replacement of those fighter leaders who did not meet his 'exacting' standards in preparation for the move of all *Jagdgeschwader* to the Pas-de-Calais.

In JG 26, Major Gotthard Handrick was replaced by Oberstleutnant Adolf Galland as *Geschwaderkommodore*, Pingel replaced Hauptmann Kurt Fischer and Hauptmann Gerhard Schöpfel took over III./JG 26 from Galland. The only JG 26 *Gruppenkommandeur* to keep his job (for the time being) was Hauptmann Erich Bode, who had only taken over II./JG 26 on 17 August following the death of Hauptmann Karl Ebbighausen the previous day. There were also a number of other changes at *Staffelkapitän* level in JG 26. The other *Jagdgeschwader*, including JG 53, were similarly affected within two weeks. Pingel, who received the *Ritterkreuz* on 14 September 1940, was subsequently shot down and taken prisoner on 10 July 1941, by which time his victories stood at 21 in World War 2. His place as *Staffelkapitän* of 2. *Staffel* was taken by Oberleutnant Ignaz Prestele.

The rest of the month must have been an anti-climax, for there were to be just three more days of activity in August before JG 53 relocated to the east. The target on the afternoon of the 24th was Portsmouth, the raid being carried out by 46 Ju 88s of KG 51 escorted by 302 fighters.

Only I. and II. *Gruppe* were involved, and there were two claims by 1. *Staffel* and one by 4. *Staffel* – all by pilots who would achieve more than five victories in 1940. Taking off from Cherbourg-East, I. *Gruppe* headed towards Portsmouth, which was reached without incident. Here, pilots found themselves comfortably above the defending RAF fighters, Hans-Karl Mayer spotting what he thought were three Hurricanes below him. Diving on the fighters, he opened fire on the leader, while the other two dived away. Mayer reported strikes on the fuselage and in and around the cockpit and, convinced the pilot was dead, he watched the RAF fighter dive away south of the Isle of Wight.

No Hurricanes were reported lost off the Isle of Wight on this day, and it is thought that Mayer's victim was in fact a Spitfire of No 609 Sqn flown by American Plt Off Andy Mamedoff. He had been bounced by an unseen German aeroplane that inflicted severe damage to his fighter, especially from a 20 mm round that entered the rear fuselage, went through the radio and all but penetrated his armour plating. With nothing more than a bruised back, Mamedoff managed to land his Spitfire at Middle Wallop, in Hampshire, the tailwheel collapsing as he touched down. Further inspection revealed that another 20 mm round had shredded half of the elevator and the whole aircraft had been peppered by 7.92 mm bullets. The Spitfire was so badly damaged that it was subsequently written off.

Meanwhile, back at 20,000 ft, 12 Spitfires of No 234 Sqn were about to attack what they thought were Do 17s but were probably Bf 110s. One pilot, Plt Off Jan Zurakowski, broke formation and attacked, but on seeing no results decided to climb back. Here, he recalls what happened next;

'I made the error of climbing to re-join the squadron – there was a loud bang as some of the escorting Me 109s managed to put a few cannon shells into my Spitfire. I lost control of elevator and rudder. My Spitfire then went slowly into a turn, stalled and ended up in a flat spin.'

Hans-Karl Mayer had spotted a lone fighter to the east of the Isle of Wight and led the whole *Staffel* after it. His first burst caused the fighter to break left and into the line of sight of Leutnant Alfred Zeis, leading the second *Schwarm*. Zeis fired a total of 56 20 mm cannon and 128 7.92 mm machine gun rounds into the enemy aircraft, which was seen to spiral down to crash on the eastern corner of the Isle of Wight. Jan Zurakowski continues his account;

'Having no controls, I had to bail out. At about 18,000 ft I slid open the canopy, climbed out of the cockpit and jumped. I soon found I was descending faster than the Spitfire, which was spinning above my head. I was afraid to open the 'chute because that would have slowed me down, risking me being hit by my spinning Spitfire. The ground was approaching fast, and when I could distinguish a man standing in a field with a gun, I decide to pull my rip cord. It was now or never. The parachute opened immediately and my Spitfire just missed me and hit the ground with a bang. A few seconds later I landed in the field next to the old man (from the Home Guard) who was armed with a double-barrelled shot+gun. He was badly shaken by the crash.'

This was Zeis' first success since 3 June, while Mayer's official total now stood at 14 confirmed victories. There was just one other claim, by Oberleutnant Günther Schulze-Blanck for a Spitfire south of

Bournemouth. 'Schubla' was now leading 4. *Staffel* and this was his third victory of the war.

If 24 August was a good day for 1. *Staffel*, the 25th was its zenith in the Battle of Britain. At the same time, however, 1./JG 53 experienced its first loss since 6 June, when Unteroffizier Paul Grond had been captured. From now on, losses would also increase for the remaining *Staffeln* and *Gruppen* of JG 53.

The target on 25 August for 37 Ju 88s of KG 51, escorted by 317 single- and twin-engined fighters, was Warmwell airfield, in Dorset. As the formation approached the English coast 1./JG 53 broke away to the west while the rest of the *Jagdgeschwader* lurked between Portland and Weymouth. However, the unit was unable to prevent Hurricanes of No 87 Sqn attacking Bf 110s on their way to escort the bombers, and then other RAF fighter squadrons intervened. Hans-Karl Mayer gained his 15th victory, a Hurricane that came down 500 yards offshore to the west of Portland – the pilot bailed out. Alfred Zeis claimed his third success, another Hurricane. In total I. *Gruppe* was credited with eight aircraft destroyed in the space of 20 minutes, all but one of them being credited to 1. *Staffel*.

II. *Gruppe* claimed two Spitfires, one of which went to Günther Schulze-Blanck, who was now just one victory short of the magical total of five.

In III. *Gruppe*, three victories were credited to Hauptmann Hans von Hahn and Oberleutnant Heinz Kunert of 8. *Staffel* (their seventh and eighth, respectively) and Leutnant Jakob Stoll of 9. *Staffel* (his sixth). It was von Hahn's last success with JG 53, as on 27 August he was posted to command I./JG 3 after Hauptmann Günther Lützow replaced Oberstleutnant Carl Vieck as *Geschwaderkommodore* of JG 3. Von Hahn's diary entry for this victory survives;

'The Spitfires approached in a long string of pearls, peeled off as if on a training flight and were about to carry out a textbook attack on our bombers. We roared into them from above; they now forgot about the bombers and instead a wild dogfight began. They tried to force us inland, but in short order they lost three of their number, which went down in flames into the sea. Then they made off. I latched onto the last one. First

Aircraft of 5./JG 53 taxi out for a massed takeoff in late August 1940. Note that they all have the recently introduced yellow nose and rudder, and some have the remains of the red band. The nearest aircraft also has two victory bars on its fin. 5. *Staffel* suffered high attrition while flying combat missions from Guernsey, having one pilot killed and two captured on 13 August and two killed 13 days later

These future aces, all then serving with II. *Gruppe*, were photographed at the end of 1939. They are, from left to right, Hauptmann Günther von Maltzahn (*Gruppenkommandeur*, 68 victories, survived), Oberleutnant Heinz Bretnütz (*Staffelkapitän* 6./JG 53, 32 victories, died on 27 June 1941 from wounds), Oberfeldwebel Werner Kauffmann (4. *Staffel*, seven victories, killed on 11 November 1940), Oberleutnant Eduard Schröder (6. *Staffel*, 29 victories, survived) and Oberfeldwebel Albrecht Baun (6. *Staffel*, five victories, killed on 25 August 1940). The latter pilot, having claimed his fifth victory – a Spitfire – on 15 August 1940 southwest of Portland at 1846 hrs, was reported missing in action ten days later. His body was never recovered

its canopy flew off, then it wobbled oddly during one burst, went straight down belching smoke and flames, and then it was nothing more than a tiny white speck of foam.'

Von Hahn survived the war with 34 victories, having been awarded the *Ritterkeruz* in 1941. His place as *Staffelkapitän* was taken by his slightly more successful deputy, Oberleutnant Heinz Kunert, who was destined to lead the *Staffel* for a mere two weeks.

There were a number of losses for I. and II. *Gruppe*. 1. *Staffel* lost a pilot on his first mission over England, while 6, *Staffel* suffered badly, with two killed and two wounded. Amongst those killed was up-and-coming ace Oberfeldwebel Albrecht Baun, who already had five victories to his credit, the last coming on 15 August. One of those wounded was former *Legion Condor* veteran Feldwebel Bernhard Seufert. Despite three victories in Spain, Seufert had failed to achieve any confirmed successes since Spain and, following his recovery from injuries, he was lost on operations off the Kent coast on 1 December 1940.

As it transpired, 26 August 1940 was the last day that JG 53 flew operations over the west of England *en masse*. III. *Gruppe* was already in the process of moving to Le Touquet, south of Boulogne, so just I. and II.

The unmistakable figure of Hans-Karl Mayer, dubbed 'Mayer-Ast' ('Lanky Mayer') by those under his command, towers over members of his 1. *Staffel* groundcrew, all of whom appear to be studying something of interest in the area of the starboard tailplane. The last two of the 17 victory bars marked on the rudder of the *Staffelkapitän*'s Emil refer to a Hurricane and Spitfire he downed near Portsmouth on 26 August

Gruppe were in action off Portsmouth that afternoon. Yet again II. Gruppe was unlucky, 5. *Staffel* losing three aircraft with two pilots killed. It was 1. *Staffel* that claimed all but one of I. *Gruppe*'s victories, with two for Hans-Karl Mayer (his 16th and 17th) and one for Alfred Zeis (his fourth). The final victory fell to Hauptmann Wolfgang Lippert of 3. *Staffel* (his tenth).

Hans-Karl Mayer made the combat look easy. He spotted five Hurricanes heading towards the He 111s of KG 55 12 miles east of Portsmouth. Singling one out, he fired just 12 20 mm cannon and 30 7.92 mm machine gun rounds and saw the Hurricane catch fire and dive away. He concluded that his victim was both young and inexperienced to allow him such an easy victory. Five minutes later he came up behind a Spitfire of No 602 Sqn flown by future ace Sgt Cyril Babbage. Babbage was too intent on attacking an He 111 to notice two Bf 109s behind him. Mayer again used minimal ammunition, and Babbage was forced to bail out of his burning fighter south of Selsey Bill.

However, 1. *Staffel* also suffered a loss when Feldwebel Heinrich Bezner's fighter suffered engine failure and dived into the Channel – his body was washed ashore at Boulogne nearly a month later. Bezner had been credited with 1. *Staffel*'s second victory of the war on 10 September 1939, but had failed to add to his score since then.

Two days later, I. *Gruppe* moved east to Neuville and II. *Gruppe* transferred to Sempy in preparation for the next phase of the Battle of Britain – the aerial assault against London. There would be a number of changes in leadership over the next month, some as a result of enemy action. The Battle of Britain was about to become harder for the aces of JG 53.

The pilots of 1./JG 53 come together for a final photograph at Cherbourg-East prior to flying east to Neuville, in the Pas-de-Calais, on 28 August 1940. They are, from left to right, Unteroffizier Willi Ghesla (PoW from 5 October 1940), Feldwebel Herbert Tzschoppe (PoW from 15 September 1940), Feldwebel Heinrich Höhnisch (PoW from 9 September 1940), Leutnant Alfred Zeis (PoW from 5 October 1940), Oblt Hans Ohly (survived), Hauptmann Hans-Karl Mayer (killed on 17 October 1940), Leutnant Ernst-Albrecht Schulz (survived), Unteroffizier Werner Karl (PoW from 2 September 1940) and Unteroffizier Heinrich Rühl (killed on 4 June 1941)

Hauptmann Wolf-Dietrich Wilcke smiles for the camera whilst strapped into his Bf 109E-4 of Stab. III./JG 53 possibly at Villiaze, on Guernsey, in August 1940

CHAPTER FOUR

BATTLE OF BRITAIN – THE EASTERN BATTLE

Bf 109E-4 'Black 14' of 2. *Staffel* is pushed back into its sandbagged and camouflage-netted revetment at Le Touquet in early September. This is believed to be the aircraft favoured by Oberfeldwebel Franz Kaiser, who claimed a Blenheim and a Hurricane destroyed on 19 and 29 September 1940 to 'make ace' – he had downed a Battle during the 'Phoney War' and a Potez 63 and another Battle during the Battle of France. Note the remnants of the red stripe beneath the nose. At first the 'red band' edict was scrupulously complied with by JG 53, but the stripes did not remain intact for long. Kaiser's aeroplane has obviously had its yellow cowling replaced at some point, leaving the red stripe around the lower panel only

B y 28 August 1940 all of JG 53 was based in or around the Pas-de-Calais, and the *Jagdgeschwader*'s first mission 'in the east' was flown the following day. According to Oberleutnant Hans Ohly's log book, he took off on a 'Freie Jagd' towards London at 1600 hrs and landed at 1720 hrs without having made any contact with the RAF. Only one victory was achieved that day, by Oberleutnant Günther Schulze-Blanck of 4. *Staffel* – a Hurricane at 1708 hrs at an unknown location. At last 'Schubla' had his fifth success, and he would add one more to this tally exactly a week later. However, within 11 days he would be dead.

On 29 August III. *Gruppe* escorted bombers towards London, with the remaining two *Gruppen* covering their return in and around Dover. This was followed on the 31st by all three *Gruppen* escorting bombers and then carrying out a 'Freie Jagd' that ended with them attacking the Dover balloon barrage and claiming to have shot down 74 blimps! There was one more escort mission undertaken that evening by all of I. and III. *Gruppen*, during which 1. *Staffel* claimed another 16 balloons over Dover. Finally, III. *Gruppe* was involved in combat with RAF fighters from 2035 hrs to 2042 hrs, Hauptmann Wolf-Dietrich Wilcke gaining his first victory of the Battle of Britain (his fourth overall) and Leutnant Erich Schmidt his second during the course of the engagement.

August 1940 ended with JG 53 not having suffered any major losses in five days, although its daily victory tally had reduced somewhat. However, this changed dramatically during the first two days of September.

Changes now occurred amongst the Executive Officers of I. *Gruppe*. On 2 September Hauptmann Hans-Karl Mayer replaced Hauptmann Albert Blumensaat as *Gruppenkommandeur* of I./JG 53, his replacement at *Staffelkapitän* of 1./JG 53 being Hans Ohly. The next day, Mayer's award of the *Ritterkreuz* was announced (the second of the war for JG 53), which coincided with Hauptmann Wolfgang Lippert being posted to command II./JG 27 – Lippert's award of the *Ritterkreuz* was announced on 24 September 1940. He was subsequently shot down over North Africa by Flt Lt Clive 'Killer' Caldwell of No 250 Sqn on 23 November 1941. Having suffered grievous wounds during this action, Lippert was soon captured and eventually passed away on 3 December 1941. His place as *Staffelkapitän* was taken by *Gruppen* Adjutant of I./JG 53, Oberleutnant Julius Haase, whose tally of confirmed victories had been stuck on four since 15 May 1940. It did not increase, as 12 days later he was shot down and killed.

By the end of September 1940, all three I. *Gruppe Staffelkapitän* who had not only flown in Spain but had also been in command since 1939 had received the *Ritterkreuz*, Hauptmann Rolf Pingel's being announced on 14 September.

Operationally, the first two days of September saw two victories for 3. *Staffel* on the 2nd (one being Wolfgang Lippert's 11th, and last, with JG 53) for the loss of five of the *Gruppe*'s Bf 109s, with one pilot captured, two missing and one wounded. Twenty-four hours earlier, II. *Gruppe* had claimed just one victory, scored by Hauptmann Günther von Maltzahn (his seventh), and suffered no losses. Most of the successes that day went to III. *Gruppe*. Around noon four fighters were claimed, both Hauptmann Wolf-Dietrich Wilcke of *Stab*. III/JG 53 and Unteroffizier Hans-Georg Schulte of 7. *Staffel* getting their fifth victories. The following day Feldwebels Herbert Schramm and Werner Stumpf from 7. *Staffel* each scored their second. By the end of 1940 Schramm had been promoted to leutnant and increased his score to eight, but Stumpf remained on just two until 22 June 1941. However, 'Stumpen' Stumpf went on to achieved greater things, and by the time of his death in North Africa on 13 October 1942 he had 48 victories to his name and had been awarded both the *Ritterkreuz* and the *Deutsches Kreuz* in Gold. But III. *Gruppe*'s successes were tempered by the loss of three aircraft on 1 September, with one pilot captured and one missing.

The next two days were uneventful for JG 53, albeit a Bf 109E-4 of 4. *Staffel* was damaged in combat on 3 September, but the pace of battle quickened again from the 5th. On this day it appears that just II. and III. *Gruppen* were in action, with Hauptmann Günther von Maltzahn (*Stab*. II./JG 53) and Hauptmann Heinz Bretnütz (6. *Staffel*) getting their sixth and 15th victories, respectively, late in the afternoon. Shortly afterwards III. *Gruppe* claimed five, Unteroffizier Hans-Georg Schulte (7. *Staffel*) getting his sixth, Oberleutnant Heinz Kunert (8. *Staffel*) his ninth, Leutnant Friedrich-Karl Müller (8. *Staffel*) his ninth and Leutnant

On 2 September Hauptmann Hans-Karl Mayer replaced Hauptmann Albert Blumensaat as *Gruppenkommandeur* of I./JG 53, his replacement at *Staffelkapitän* of 1./JG 53 being Hans Ohly. The next day, Mayer's award of the *Ritterkreuz* was announced (the second of the war for JG 53), and he is seen here in his official photograph wearing the award around his neck

Erich Schmidt (9. *Staffel*) his third. However, three Bf 109s were lost by III. *Gruppe*, with one pilot missing and another captured.

There was one more curious loss on 5 September. Fifty-one-year-old Hauptmann Wilhelm Meyerweissflog (who had been an observer with the German air force in World War 1) had been attached to *Stab./JG 53*, in what capacity is uncertain, and had flown on operations on a number of occasions. For example, on 26 August he was flying as *Rottenflieger* to Oberleutnant Gebhard Dittmar in 1. *Staffel's Deckungsschwarm*. Having returned from leave during the evening of 5 September, he spotted a large number of aircraft taking off and decided to join them. Jumping in his Bf 109E-1, he flew alone vaguely in the direction of England until he was picked off by a Spitfire, probably flown by experienced Australian ace Flg Off Pat Hughes of No 234 Sqn. With an overheating engine, Meyerweissflog was forced to crash-land near Manston, in Kent, and was duly taken prisoner. He was eventually repatriated in 1944.

During 6 September JG 53 flew three missions, resulting in the capture of the *Geschwader's* first ace in the Battle of Britain. The day was relatively quiet for I. *Gruppe*, its new *Gruppenkommandeur*, Hans-Karl Mayer, being credited with a Hurricane northwest of Dungeness on the first mission in the morning (his 18th). His Adjutant, Oberleutnant Gebhard Dittmar, was lost somewhere in the Hastings area, however. He was replaced by Oberleutnant Heinz-Eugen Wittmeyer, whose time in this post would last just two days, and his loss would involve the death of another 'Pik-As' ace.

In II. *Gruppe* four victories were achieved in the first mission, all to successful pilots, namely Hauptmann Günther von Maltzahn (his seventh), Oberleutnant Günther Schulze-Blanck (his sixth), Feldwebel Werner Kauffmann (his fifth) and Hauptmann Heinz Bretnütz (his 16th). Apparently, 'Schubla' Schulze-Blanck suffered slight wounds when his fighter was hit in the cockpit by gunfire which caused 30 per cent damage to the aircraft. At the same time III. *Gruppe* claimed three aircraft, Oberleutnant Jakob Stoll, *Staffelkapitän* of 9./JG 53 shooting down his seventh and Oberleutnant Friedrich-Karl Müller of 8. *Staffel* his tenth.

Little appears to have happened on the second mission of the day, but the last operation resulted in the loss of two experienced III. *Gruppe* pilots. Oberleutnant Hans Ohly of 1. *Staffel* recorded that he took off at 1818 hrs to escort Bf 109 *Jabos*. A short, sharp and inconclusive combat occurred, but all pilots returned safely. However, III. *Gruppe* pilots tangled with what they reported as being 40-50 Spitfires in the Tilbury-Southend area. The Bf 109 flown by Feldwebel Ernst Hempel of 8. *Staffel* was seen to explode, and its remains, together with its dead pilot, came down in the River Medway. Meanwhile, Oberleutnant Helmut Riegel, *Staffelkapitän* of 7./JG 53, simply disappeared, and it is believed that his fighter came down in the Thames Estuary too. Riegel was quickly replaced by Leutnant Heinz Altendorf, who already had four victories to his name but none so far in the Battle of Britain.

The final casualty of the day was 22-year-old ace Unteroffizier Hans-Georg Schulte of 7./JG 53. Other members of his *Staffel* reported that they had been involved in a dogfight over the Thames Estuary, and that shortly after seeing him shoot down a Spitfire at 1810 hrs British time for his eighth victory of the war, Schulte's fighter was damaged in combat (by either Sgt Edward Darling of No 41 Sqn or Sgt Ian Hutchinson or Plt Off Tim Vigors of No 222 Sqn – both Darling and Vigors later became aces) and he force-landed at Manston. Captured unhurt, he revealed very little when interrogated, and the RAF never really realised how successful this pilot had been despite his lowly rank.

2./JG 53's 'Black 4' was also photographed at Le Touquet in the autumn of 1940 sat in its recently built sandbagged and camouflage-netted revetment. Behind it, four more 'Emils' are being readied for their next mission across the Channel

The first major daylight attack on London was launched on 7 September and, understandably, JG 53 formed part of the escort. I. *Gruppe* flew two missions, the only claim being by Hans-Karl Mayer on the second – his score now stood at 19. There were no victories for II. *Gruppe* and just two on the second mission for III. *Gruppe*. The *Geschwader* suffered no losses, but this would not be the case the following day, as recounted by *Gruppe* Adjutant Oberleutnant Heinz Wittmeyer of *Stab.* I./JG 53;

'The order of the day for the *Gruppe* was to fly close escort for a *Gruppe* of He 111s heading to the east of London. Flying at about 20,000 ft before crossing the coast between Dungeness and Hastings, I spotted three fighters north-northwest and reported this to Hauptmann Mayer. He gave the order for the *Gruppe* to turn towards them. Being three aircraft, we thought it was the enemy, but soon after they were identified as Bf 109s. They were at exactly the same altitude as the *Gruppenschwarm* and headed straight towards us. Normally, they would give way, as we were in a *Gruppe* formation – two of them did, passing underneath us, but the third didn't. I tried at the very last second to avoid disaster, but it was too late. Both Bf 109s disintegrated and I found myself in open air. A little later I opened my parachute – I was more or less blind in my right eye (later, in a field hospital, a specialist removed more than 20 metal splinters). The other pilot did not get out.

Unteroffizier Hans-Georg Schulte's Bf 109E-4 Wk-Nr 1506 of 7./JG 53 crash-landed near Manston on 6 September 1940 after he was attacked by either Sgt Edward Darling of No 41 Sqn or Sgt Ian Hutchinson or Plt Off Tim Vigors of No 222 Sqn. Seen here being put on display in central London some weeks later, the fighter's distinctly tatty white cowling bears no sign of a red band – there is no swastika on the tailfin either. The latter has clearly been overpainted, which was III. *Gruppe*'s collective response to the loss of the 'Ace of Spades' *Geschwader* badge. Most pilots utilised the space thus made available to display their scoreboard, although it appears that Schulte has only recorded two of his six previous victories (a seventh was credited to him during his final mission) on the fin of this aeroplane

Unteroffizier Hans-Georg Schulte as a PoW in Canada in September 1943. He was credited with seven victories (an eighth remained unconfirmed) between 14 May and 6 September 1940. He was one of four pilots lost by JG 53 on the latter date, the remaining three being killed

'Later, I was told that the *Staffel* to which the three Bf 109s belonged had been involved in combat over London. The *Staffel* had suffered losses and broke up, and they were on their way back. The pilot of the one that collided with me was probably looking backwards to be sure of not being attacked again, and did not see us in time. It seems that one blade of his propeller cut my cockpit in front of my head and the next blade behind my head, cutting the seat belt.'

In addition to Wittmeyer, there were two other losses suffered by JG 53 that day. One was an aircraft of 3./JG 53 that crashed near Sevenoaks, in Kent, killing its pilot, and the other was the fighter flown by 26-year-old Oberleutnant Heinz Kunert, *Staffelkapitän* of 8./JG 53, who had collided with Wittmeyer. His body was later washed ashore at Cap Gris Nez. Kunert had shot down nine aircraft, the last of these having been claimed three days earlier.

There were a number of claims made on 8 September, notably by Oberleutnant Ignaz Prestele of 2. *Staffel* (his fifth) and recently promoted Oberleutnant Franz Götz of 9. *Staffel* (his sixth). Later in the day Leutnant Heinz Altendorf of 7. *Staffel* shot down a Blenheim, which was his first victory of the Battle of Britain and his fifth overall. Thus, JG 53 now had two more pilots with five victories to their credit, but the following day saw the demise of two more experienced pilots.

The *Jagdgeschwader* was again busy on 9 September, but not until the afternoon. Just before 1800 hrs, 1. *Staffel* set off on an escort sortie to London and claimed three aircraft, one falling to Hans-Karl Mayer to take his tally to 20. However, 1. *Staffel* in turn lost one of its successful pilots. Feldwebel Heinrich Höhnisch, who was due to celebrate his 23rd birthday in eight days' time, already had six victories to his name, his last being claimed on 13 August. Here, he relates what happened to him on the evening of the 9th September;

'Our mission was to give fighter cover to the rear of an He 111 formation. One *Kette* of three He 111s had become separated, so 1. *Staffel* was forced to escort them with seven Bf 109s. My position was the *Deckungsrotte* with Oberfeldwebel Alfred Müller.

Oberleutnant Ignaz Prestele, *Staffelkapitan* of 2./JG 53, relaxes between flights outside a personnel shelter at Le Touquet in the early autumn of 1940. Having claimed four victories in Spain with 1./J 88 in 1937-38, Prestele was credited with single successes during the 'Phoney War' and Battle of France (both RAF Battles) and four Hurricanes in September 1940. Seven more victories followed during the early stages of Operation *Barbarossa*, and he then returned to the west to become *Gruppenkommandeur* of I./JG 2. Prestele claimed a Hampden destroyed on 12 February 1942, which went unconfirmed, and was subsequently killed in action fighting Spitfires of the Biggin Hill Wing on 4 May that same year, his Bf 109F crashing into the Channel off the French coast north of Le Havre

'Approaching London Docks, there was no enemy contact. I felt sure that we would be attacked out of the sun as soon as we had turned 180 degrees for our return flight, but to my surprise I saw when looking ahead six Spitfires on an opposite track about 50 m above. To avoid the inevitable attack I tried to close up with my *Staffel* flying ahead and below me, and when I was level with my *Staffelkapitän* I thought I had made it. However, there was a rattle like an explosion in my 'plane and I felt flames like a blowtorch hit my face. Under great difficulty I made it out of the cockpit, but with severe burns to my face and hands and bullet wounds to my right thigh.'

Höhnisch was probably shot down by Kiwi ace Flt Lt Wilf Clouston of No 19 Sqn, who wrote;

'Just as I was about to attack [seven Bf 110s], two Me 109s crossed my sights, so I turned onto them. The rear one emitted glycol fumes after a short burst and then burst into flames.'

Höhnisch was the sole casualty in I. *Gruppe*, while II. *Gruppe* claimed nothing but lost Oberleutnant Günther Schulze-Blanck, a former *Legion Condor* pilot and *Staffelkapitän* of 4./JG 53 with six victories to his name. His friend, Leutnant Erich Bodendiek, destined to be shot down and taken prisoner himself nine days later, remembers what happened:

'The wounds that "Schubla" received on 6 September were not significant and he was flying again two days or so after. "Schubla" was very popular – he was a happy-go-lucky type and looked like a younger version of German film star Hans Albers. I remember it was 9 September that he was shot down. He suddenly turned his 'plane and dived, shouting over the radio, "I'm following a Spitfire! Follow me!" But we could not, as he was going too fast, and then we lost him as there were 30 or 40 aeroplanes around. Then his voice came though, "Help, Help! I'm wounded – they have hit me." That was all.'

The body of 25-year-old 'Schubla' was washed ashore in France 20 days later, and he was posthumously promoted to hauptmann. He was replaced as *Staffelkapitän* by Oberleutnant Richard Vogel, who had three victories and would get a fourth on 11 September, only to be killed in action off Ramsgate on 10 October.

Meanwhile, in III. *Gruppe,* the four victories claimed on the 9th went to 9. *Staffel*, Oberleutnant Jakob Stoll taking his score to nine by shooting down two Spitfires and Leutnant Erich Schmidt gaining his fourth. One pilot from 8. *Staffel* was killed in action.

The Battle of Britain was now five days away from its crescendo, but for JG 53 the days preceding 15 September were relatively quiet. In I. *Gruppe* just two victories were claimed, both on the afternoon of the 12th. One, a Blenheim that fell to Leutnant Alfred Zeis of 1. *Staffel*, took this pilot's tally to five, but by his own admission his victory was dubious;

'I had been on a ferry flight from Rennes to Le Touquet and was flying along the coast. The weather was bad, with almost total low cloud. Just before I reached Le Havre I saw splashes on the edge of the harbour and saw three 'planes headed for the cloud, one after the other. At full throttle I tried to intercept before

Leutnant Heinz Altendorf took command of 7. *Staffel* following the death of Oberleutnant Hans Riegel on 6 September. The latter, who had led 7./JG 53 since 18 May 1940, disappeared over the Thames Estuary near Tilbury. Altendorf had been credited with four victories during the Battle of France, and he added two more to his tally on 8 (Blenheim) and 20 (Spitfire) September. He remained *Staffelkapitän* until 20 February 1942, when he was forced down behind British lines in Libya after his fighter was hit by flak. By then Altendorf had claimed 24 victories

The second ace to be lost on 9 September was Feldwebel Heinrich Höhnisch (left) of 1. *Staffel*, who was attacked by a Spitfire (probably a No 19 Sqn machine flown by Kiwi ace Flt Lt Wilf Clouston) whilst escorting He 111s targeting London docks. Höhnisch, who had six victories to his name, recalled 'there was a rattle like an explosion in my 'plane and I felt flames like a blowtorch hit my face. Under great difficulty I made it out of the cockpit, but with severe burns to my face and hands and bullet wounds to my right thigh.' Both he and his aeroplane came down near Biggin Hill

The grave of Oberleutnant Günther Schulze-Blanck, *Staffelkapitän* of 4./JG 53, who was reported missing on 9 September 1940. His body was washed ashore on the French coast some 20 days later. A veteran of combat in Spain with J 88 (although he failed to score any victories with the unit), Schulze-Blanck became an ace between 13 August and 6 September 1940. Slightly wounded when his cockpit was hit by machine gun fire on the latter date, Schulze-Blanck chased after a Spitfire whilst escorting bombers targeting London on the afternoon of the 9th and was in turn bounced and shot down

they reached the cloud, and just before the last one disappeared I expended all of my 20 mm ammunition against him, without success – the range was too great. I followed the last 'plane into cloud, flying on instruments, and came up behind three Blenheims flying close together. I first shot at the engines of the left-hand Blenheim, and then attacked the right-hand one before they disappeared into cloud, but not before my Messerschmitt had received several hits in return. Before they disappeared I saw the effect of some of my fire, which was black smoke coming from one of the 'planes.'

The Blenheims were from No 59 Sqn, which reported being attacked by a Bf 109 at 1620 hrs, which corresponds with Zeis' claim. They did not report hitting the German fighter, but said that one of the Blenheims returned with damage to a propeller and its fuselage. Zeis was credited with the victory on 9 November 1940, by which time he was a PoW. After the war he said of the combat;

'In my combat report I stated that at least one Blenheim had been damaged, but when I was asked I did not completely exclude a kill, but as none of those Blenheims had been hit by 20 mm ammunition I felt that a kill was questionable.'

During the same four-day period II. *Gruppe* reported just two victories on 11 September, with no losses. As usual, however, III. *Gruppe* averred to have done better, with five claims on the evening of 11 September and one on the 14th (the first for Gefreiter Rolf Klippgen, who would go on to claim another 17 before being killed in action on 19 February 1944 while commanding 7./JG 53).

The claims on 11 September are worth mentioning as they were for three biplanes (one by the *Gruppenkommandeur* Hauptmann Wolf-Dietrich Wilcke for his sixth victory) and two Blenheims (one of which was the tenth victory for Oberleutnant Jakob Stoll). That evening, five Blenheims of No 53 Sqn and six from No 59 Sqn, accompanied by Fleet Air Arm Fairey Albacores of 826 Naval Air Squadron and escorted by Blenheims of No 235 Sqn, had attacked a convoy off Calais. Together with III./JG 53, I./JG 52 claimed four Albacores and four Blenheims destroyed. Actual losses were one Albacore shot down and three damaged and two Blenheims of No 235 Sqn listed as missing. Although the British crews had claimed to have shot down three Bf 109s and damaged a Do 18, the only loss was of a Bf 109 from I./JG 52 to an unknown cause.

Now recognised as Battle of Britain Day, 15 September 1940 did not start for JG 53 until just before midday. In the morning I. *Gruppe* moved to its new airfield at Etaples, and then the whole *Geschwader* took off just after 1100 hrs to form part of the escort for Do 17s of I. and II./KG 76 attacking London. It proved to be a brutal day, with Hans-Karl Mayer claiming his 21st and 22nd victories (the 22nd destined to be his last confirmed success) as I./JG 53 downed four aircraft. At the same time, it lost five fighters, including that of Oberleutnant Julius Haase, *Staffelkapitän* of 3./JG 53. Another loss was Oberfeldwebel Alfred 'Molinero' Müller, who was leading 1. *Staffel* after Oberleutnant Hans Ohly turned back with radio failure. Müller, another ex-*Legion Condor* pilot, was heard to say he was wounded in the arm and was turning for home. It is believed he came down in the Channel and was later captured. It appears he was later repatriated, as he died of peritonitis in a hospital in Germany on 18 June 1944.

Haase was replaced by Oberleutnant Walter Rupp, formerly of 1. *Staffel*, who had just returned after recovering from injuries sustained when he and Unteroffizier Ludwig Reibel collided on 10 May. Rupp was to last just one month and two days, as his Bf 109 was damaged in combat during a *Jabo* mission and he was captured after making a forced landing at Manston.

No claims or losses were filed by II. *Gruppe* on 15 September, but yet again III. *Gruppe* reported doing well. On its first mission of the day the unit credited six victories to pilots who had, or would achieve, five or more kills – Leutnant Erich Schmidt (9. *Staffel*, victories five and six), Oberleutnant Jakob Stoll (9. *Staffel*, victories 11 and 12), Feldwebel Herbert Schramm (7. *Staffel*, third victory) and Oberleutnant Wolf-Dietrich Wilcke (*Stab*. III./JG 53, seventh victory). It did lose two aircraft, however. Ace Oberleutnant Friedrich-Karl 'Tutti' Müller, formerly of 8. *Staffel* and now flying with *Stab*. III/JG 53, ran out of fuel and was forced to ditch in the Channel – it is uncertain whether this incident took place on the first mission or not. He was quickly rescued. Another fighter was written off in a crash-landing back at Etaples.

A second mission, apparently a 'Freie Jagd' by the whole *Geschwader*, occurred later in the afternoon, and 1. *Staffel* reported getting airborne at 1445 hrs. Five victories without loss were claimed by I. *Gruppe*, Oberleutnant Ignaz Prestele getting his sixth, while III. *Gruppe* claimed another four, to Hauptmann Wolf-Dietrich Wilcke (two Spitfires), Oberleutnant Jakob Stoll and Leutnant Erich Schmidt. It too suffered no losses.

There was a final mission for I. and III. *Gruppen* that day. The latter unit was scrambled to intercept Blenheims, and Feldwebel Hermann

Seen here in late 1942 after receiving the *Ritterkreuz* and *Eichenlaub*, future 139-victory ace Oberleutnant Friedrich-Karl Müller flew with both 8. *Staffel* and *Stab*. III./JG 53 in 1940. Although he claimed eight victories during the Battle of France, he enjoyed little success during the Battle of Britain – he claimed single Spitfires on 5 and 6 September, but only one (the latter, over Dungeness) was confirmed. On 15 September, shortly after transferring to *Stab*. III./JG 53, Müller was forced to ditch in the Channel when he ran out of fuel. Subsequently fighting on the Eastern Front and in North Africa with I./JG 53, before undertaking Defence of the Reich missions with IV./JG 3, he was killed in a flying accident on 29 May 1944 whilst *Kommodore* of JG 3. By then Müller had flown more than 600 combat sorties

Oberleutnant Ignaz Prestele sits strapped into the cockpit of his Bf 109E-4 'Black 2' at Le Touquet, both he and his mechanic awaiting the signal to start up the fighter's DB 601 engine prior to taxiing out for takeoff

Hauptmann Hans-Karl Mayer kept his 'White 8' after taking command of I. *Gruppe* on 31 August 1940. On the rudder are 29 victory bars, 22 of them for manned aircraft (the last two coming on 15 September) and those adorned with a circle denoting a barrage balloon destroyed

Neuhoff of 7./JG 53 claimed to have shot one down (for his ninth victory) 18 miles northwest of Etaples. It has not been possible to ascertain who or what he attacked.

The losses suffered by I. *Gruppe* in particular hit JG 53 hard, with Hauptmann Mayer's report for victory confirmation for him and his pilots following this mission hinting at the strain the *Jagdgeschwader* was now coming under following the Luftwaffe's switch to bombing targets in and around London;

'There are no certain witnesses for the victories because in the air fighting on this day the defence had to break up into individual combats in the face of superior numbers of English fighters. A large number of aircraft were observed going down in flames by several members of the *Gruppe*. In no case was it possible to observe precisely by whom and how these were shot down.'

Although there was a lull in the action following Battle of Britain Day, the 'Pik-As' *Geschwader* still engaged the RAF, albeit with less intensity. First thing in the morning on 16 September Hauptmann Han-Karl Mayer led JG 53 on an escort mission, although poor weather meant no contact with Fighter Command. It appears that Mayer then went on leave, as temporary leadership of I. *Gruppe* passed to Hans Ohly. Contemporary photos of Mayer show how tired he now looked, and he was not to return to the Channel until on or about 11 October. Six days later he would be dead.

Hauptmann Wolf-Dietrich Wilcke taxies his Bf 109E-4 out of its blast pen at Le Touquet, the *Gruppenkommandeur* of III./JG 53 being sent on his way with crisp salutes from his fellow officers in the foreground. Between 31 August and 10 October 1940 Wilcke was credited with ten victories and one unconfirmed kill

Another successful pilot died on 17 September – it seems that the *Geschwader* undertook a number of 'Freie Jagd' on that date. I. *Gruppe* flew between 1550 hrs and 1712 hrs without incident, while II. *Gruppe* reported two fighters slightly damaged in combat. III. *Gruppe*'s 'Freie Jagd' must have partly coincided with I. and II./JG 53, as between 1640 and 1650 hrs the unit claimed two Spitfires and a Hurricane destroyed. Two of the successful pilots were again Leutnant Erich Schmidt and Hauptmann Wolf-Dietrich Wilcke. RAF fighters from Nos 41, 303 and 603 Sqns claimed four Bf 109s destroyed, five probably destroyed and two damaged, but the only losses at that time were three from 9./JG 53.

Unteroffizier Manfred Langer, who had been with 9. *Staffel* for just one month and two days, was killed when his fighter was shot down by ace Plt Off George 'Ben' Bennions of No 41 Sqn and crashed into a wood between Faversham and Canterbury, in Kent. *Staffelkapitän* Oberleutnant Jakob Stoll and Oberleutnant Herbert Seliger were also reported missing over the Thames Estuary. Little is known about Seliger, but Stoll was one of the most successful pilots of the *Geschwader*, with 13 confirmed victories. What happened to him is uncertain, but RAF pilots reported seeing two Bf 109s collide when bounced and then spin away, presumably to crash. Neither pilot's body was washed ashore, and command of 9. *Staffel* now went to the experienced former NCO Oberleutnant Franz Götz, who celebrated the next day by shooting down a Spitfire for his eighth confirmed victory of the war.

The remainder of September 1940 brought mixed fortunes for JG 53. Oberleutnant Hans Ohly lists 15 *Feindflug* (combat sorties) between 18 and 29 September, the busiest days being the 18th, 24th and 27th, when he flew three *Feindflug* per day. Just seven victories were achieved by I. *Gruppe* during this period. The first went to Oberfeldwebel Franz Kaiser of 2. *Staffel* on the evening of 19 September. Kaiser had not shot anything down since 27 May (his third victory of the war), but at 1725 hrs he despatched a Blenheim south of Hastings. His victim is thought to have been from No 53 Sqn and flown by 23-year-old New Zealander Plt Off Clarence Tibbitts, who had taken off from Detling, in Kent, at 1600 hrs German time and was believed lost off Berck-sur-Mer.

Kaiser was subsequently one of five successful I. *Gruppe* pilots to down RAF fighters on 29 September, thus achieving his fifth victory – he would not claim another aircraft in 1940. The other noteworthy pilot on this day was his *Staffelkapitän*, Oberleutnant Ignaz Prestele, who shot down two Hurricanes to increase his score to eight. He too would then endure a lean spell until 1941. In fact, I. *Gruppe* would achieve only three victories between 28 September 1940 and 26 April 1941! Conversely, it was to lose just one more pilot and aircraft between 16 and 30 September.

In the last 13 days of September 1940 II. *Gruppe* claimed 12 RAF fighters for two pilots captured and three aircraft lost. One of the pilots lost, on 30 September, was Unteroffizier Josef Wurmheller of 5. *Staffel*. A pre-war pilot with 2./JG 53, 'Sepp' Wurmheller claimed his first victory on the 30th September 1939, after which he was posted away to be an instructor. He returned to join 5./JG 53 in the early summer of 1940, but had to wait until 28 September 1940 for his second victory. He was uninjured as a result of his ditching 48 hours later, and on 16 October he

Following the death of 13-victory ace Oberleutnant Jakob Stoll on 17 September (along with two other pilots from (9./JG 53), fellow *experte* Oberleutnant Franz Götz – seen here trying to catch up with his sleep between missions – took over command of 9. *Staffel*. He had nine victories to his name by the end of the year, and would eventually rise to command III./JG 53. Credited with at least 55 victories, and having also seen combat on the Eastern Front, North Africa and Italy, Götz ended the war as *Kommodore* of JG 26. He subsequently served in the post-war Luftwaffe

Feldwebel Franz Kaiser of 2. *Staffel* took almost exactly a year to 'make ace', claiming his first success on 30 September 1939 and his fifth on 29 September 1940. He was credited with a sixth on 24 July 1941 and that was the end of his aerial success, for Kaiser was forced to ditch off Malta on 21 April 1942 after being attacked by future Australian ace Sgt 'Tim' Goldsmith of No 126 Sqn. He spent the rest of the war as a PoW

Following the example set by his *Gruppenkommandeur*, Feldwebel Herbert Schramm of 7./JG 53 was credited with seven victories between 2 September and 17 October 1940, earning him promotion to leutnant. By the time he was killed in action fighting USAAF P-47s on 1 December 1943 whilst serving with 5./JG 27, his victory tally had increased to 40 confirmed and five unconfirmed (*SPK*)

Bf 109E-1 WkNr 5175 'White 12' of 7./JG 53 was shot down by a Spitfire near Strood, in Kent, on 30 September 1940 and Unteroffizier Ernst Poschnreider captured. Earlier photos show this aircraft with eight victory bars, as it had previously been flown by Feldwebel Hermann Neuhoff prior to him being issued with a newer E-4 in mid-September 1940

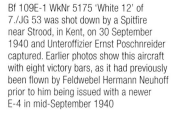

shot down his fifth, and last, aeroplane of the year. He was forced to ditch once again on 23 November, this time with more serious consequences.

As usual, III. *Gruppe* appeared to do better, with 15 victories and one pilot taken prisoner, although Oberleutnant Walter Radlick, the *Gruppen* Adjutant, also force-landed at Wissant on 23 September. He escaped injury, but his aircraft was written off. Radlick would not be so lucky nine days later. Most of the names of all but two of the successful pilots were well known. Hauptmann Wolf-Dietrich Wilcke claimed three (taking his score to 12), Leutnant Erich Schmidt claimed two (taking his score to ten), Feldwebel Herbert Schramm claimed three (taking his score to six), Oberleutnant Franz Götz claimed two (taking his score to nine) and Leutnant Heinz Altendorf claimed one (taking his score to six). The only unusual claim filed during this period was that by Feldwebel Herbert Schramm of 7./JG 53 on 26 September. He was credited with a Handley Page Hereford (a variant of the Hampden) in the early afternoon, but no loss can be positively matched to his claim. It could have been a Blenheim of No 114 Sqn, flown by Sgt Frank Wheeler, that went missing on a reconnaissance mission off Boulogne that day. Wheeler's body was recovered from the sea off the Isle of Wight on 18 October 1940.

The intensive phases of the Battle of Britain were now over, and for the remaining three months of the year victories began to tail off (just two for I. *Gruppe* and 15 for III. *Gruppe*, but a surprising 31 for II. *Gruppe*). Losses included a *Gruppenkommandeur* and four *Staffelkapitäne*, as well as five pilots who had achieved ace status before the *Geschwader* withdrew to Germany between 19 and 21 December 1940.

CHAPTER FIVE

1940 – THE FINAL DAYS

owards the end of September 1940, following 3., 4. and 8. *Staffeln* of JG 53 being designated the *Jabostaffeln*, the number of Bf 109 *Jabo* sorties increased dramatically. The first JG 53 *Jabo* mission was on 2 October, 1. *Staffel* recording three escort sorties for 'Bf 109 bombers', one mission in the morning and two in the afternoon. Four victories were claimed by two pilots from 9. *Staffel*, Leutnant Erich Schmidt and Unteroffizier Robert Wolfgarten. This took Schmidt's score to 12, while recent arrival Wolfgarten now had three (his first being scored on 30 September 1940). However, Wolfgarten gained no more victories prior to his death in an accident on 14 April 1941.

On the minus side, III. *Gruppe* suffered badly, losing four aircraft during the morning mission of 2 October. The *Gruppen* Adjutant, Oberleutnant Walter Radlick, who had four victories to his name, was shot down and killed, while Oberleutnant Walter Fiel, who had been posted in from *Stab*. I./JG 3 to lead 8. *Staffel* following the death of Oberleutnant Heinz Kunert on 8 September, was shot down and captured. His score also stood at four. The remaining two casualties were also from 8.(*Jabo*)/JG 53, Oberleutnant Siegfried Stronk (two victories) being killed and newly arrived Gefreiter Heinz Zag captured.

Owing to poor weather, the next *Jabo* escort mission was not flown until the late morning of 5 October. The target for the Bf 110-equipped specialist *Jabo* unit 1. and 2./*Eprobungsgruppe* 210 was Becton gasworks

Leutnant Alfred Zeis of 1./JG 53 poses with 'White 4' at Le Touquet just days before he was shot down – possibly by Flt Lt G R McGregor or Flg Off Paul Pitcher of Hurricane-equipped No 1 Sqn (RCAF), Zeis potentially being his fifth victim – and captured on 5 October 1940. By then Zeis had been credited with five victories

Leutnant Erich Schmidt of 9. *Staffel* did not achieve his first victory until 12 August 1940, but by 30 November that year his score stood at 17. This photograph was taken in Russia just after he had received his *Ritterkreuz*, Schmidt having increased his tally to 47 by the time he was downed by flak on 31 August 1941. He bailed out over enemy territory and was never heard from again

Leutnant Zeis's Bf 109E-4 Wk-Nr 1564 'White 3' sits in a sandbagged revetment at Le Touquet just days before it was shot down on 5 October 1940. It displays ten victory bars, including five barrage balloons and the Blenheim that 'got away' on 12 September

and West Malling airfield, in Kent. Just after crossing the coast the formation was intercepted and, as Oberleutnant Hans Ohly later wrote, there was an 'air battle with many Spitfires and Hurricanes'. Flying with Ohly was 21-year-old Austrian Leutnant Alfred Zeis, who had claimed his fifth victory on 12 September. He almost got his sixth during this mission, as he subsequently recalled;

'The *Staffel* was surprised by fighters and broke up, and we were forced to fight individually. In the course of this I shot at a Hurricane which was flying below me and attacking another Bf 109. I saved the Bf 109 from this dangerous situation but was then attacked from behind and was hit in the engine, radiator and ailerons. My *Rottenflieger* couldn't follow me and I tried, as best I could with my severely damaged 'plane, to get away, but got hit again during different evasive actions. Finally, after a turn, the 'plane went into a spin, and because of the battle damage I could not regain control, so I was forced to bail out.'

Zeis' favourite Bf 109E-4, Wk-Nr 1464, coded 'White 3', smashed into the ground near Pluckley, in Kent. The RAF could see that as well as 'White 3' on the fuselage, the fighter had a yellow nose and rudder. What they could not see was that the rudder was decorated with ten victory bars, Zeis having seen considerable action during the previous five months;

'I flew on every mission my *Staffel* performed over France in the spring of 1940 and during the French campaign that followed, as well as all the missions sent over England until I was shot down on 5 October – altogether, more than 100 missions. I had five confirmed victories and had shot down five balloons, and had been awarded the *Eisernes Kreuz* [Iron Cross] first and second classes.'

Exactly who shot down Zeis is uncertain, as the RAF claimed 13 Bf 109s destroyed, ten damaged and two probables on 5 October. German losses were six Bf 109s destroyed and two damaged during the whole day – JG 53 suffered one more from 1. *Staffel* with the pilot captured, while the aircraft flown by recently promoted Oberleutnant Heinz Altendorf, *Staffelkapitän* of 7./JG 53, was badly damaged in combat and written off in a crash-landing at Cap Gris Nez. However, a possible victor was Flg Off Paul Pitcher of No 1 Sqn (RCAF), as he relates;

'My log book reveals: 5 Oct 40, Hurricane coded YO-D. Patrol base and Dover, Me 109s and 110s engaged – one Me 109 destroyed. Engaged and damaged Me 110, port fuel tank hit. It was an extremely busy hour and five minutes and positive recollection of details is difficult. However, as far as I can recall the 109's undercarriage dropped down. My most vivid impression of that sortie was the landing at base. My aircraft was not equipped with self-sealing fuel tanks and my port fuel tank had been riddled with bullet holes and the cockpit was awash with fuel. The turbulence on landing caused clouds of fuel to swirl over the engine cowling and hot exhaust stacks and by some miracle the whole aircraft failed to explode.'

Pitcher's combat report also stated that the Bf 109's undercarriage dropped down and it then rolled onto its back south of Maidstone.

Fighter Command reported losing two Hurricanes and a Spitfire in this action, with two pilots wounded and one killed. The Luftwaffe claimed five RAF fighters, all but one being credited to pilots from JG 53, notably Hauptmann Heinz Bretnütz (victory 17) of 6./JG 53 and Oberfeldwebel Werner Kauffmann (victory seven) of 4./JG 53, and yet again Leutnant Erich Schmidt of 9./JG 53 (his 13th victory). The missions later in the day were much less eventful, although Feldwebel Herbert Schramm of 7. *Staffel* claimed his seventh victory that evening.

The following period was again quiet, with I. *Gruppe* reporting little of consequence for the next 12 days. Likewise, III. *Gruppe* was credited with just three victories, two to Leutnant Erich Schmidt on 7 and 10 October and one to Hauptmann Wolf-Dietrich Wilcke on the latter date, their tallies now being 15 and 13, respectively.

More was going on in II. *Gruppe*. On 30 September Oberstleutnant Hans-Jürgen von Cramon was posted to a staff job in Berlin and on 9 October Major Günther von Maltzahn assumed command of the *Geschwader*, celebrating his promotion by shooting down a Hurricane three days later (for his 11th victory). However, von Maltzahn had to wait

This is believed to be the recently delivered Bf 109E-7 that was flown by Hauptmann Hans-Karl Mayer on his last flight on 17 October 1940. The exact circumstances that led to the ace's demise remain unclear to this day

until 30 December before his award of the *Ritterkreuz* was announced. Hauptmann Heinz Bretnütz now became *Gruppenkommandeur* of II./JG 53, his place as *Staffelkapitän* of 6./JG 53 being taken by Oberleutnant Otto Böhner, who moved from *Stab*. II./JG 53. Although Böhner was an experienced pilot, Bretnütz with his 17 victories would be a hard act to follow, especially as Böhner had to wait until 15 November to get his first victory. Bretnütz celebrated his new command with his 18th victory on 11 October, and the announcement of his *Ritterkreuz* came on the 22nd of that same month, two days after his 20th victory.

There had also been other moves within II. *Gruppe*. Oberleutnant Rudolf Goy, *Staffelkapitän* of 5./JG 53, had been posted to 1./*Jagdfliegerschule* 5 at the start of September 1940, his place being filled by Oberleutnant Kürt Brändle. Despite his experience, and three victories in Spain, Goy had failed to shoot anything down since 27 May, whilst Brändle's score stood at five. The other change came as a result of the death of Oberleutnant Richard Vogel, *Staffelkapitän* of 4./JG 53, on 10 October. Vogel (four victories) was replaced by Oberleutnant Kurt Liedke, who would have to wait until he went to Russia to add to his sole victory of 20 September 1939, and not before he had been wounded in a strafing attack at Arques on 15 April 1941.

In addition to those mentioned previously, there were other successes for II. *Gruppe* between 5 and 17 October, notably for Unteroffizier Josef Wurmheller. For reasons that are unclear, 5. *Staffel* had moved back to Normandy at the end of September 1940, and on 12 October Wurmheller claimed a Spitfire 35 miles north of Brest, followed four days later by a Blenheim north-northeast of the Ile d'Ouessant, which took his total to five. However, despite the accuracy of the location, Wurmheller's claims cannot be substantiated. He did not score again until 4 April 1941, as he was wounded in action on 23 November 1940 and forced to ditch in the Channel.

After three generally quiet days owing to poor weather, there was a resumption of intense aerial activity on 17 October. At 0940 hrs 1. *Staffel* took off to escort Oberleutnant Walter Rupp's 3./JG 53 on a *Jabo* mission, and it appears that II. and III. *Gruppen* did the same for their respective *Jabo Staffel*, with Feldwebel Herbert Schramm of 7. *Staffel* claiming a Spitfire off Dungeness on the way back. A second mission was flown that afternoon, but it quickly began to go wrong when the aircraft attempted to return home. Bounced by RAF fighters, Oberleutnant Walter Rupp's fighter was hit by a burst of gunfire, probably from the Spitfire flown by future ace Plt Off Bryan Draper of No 74 Sqn, and the Messerschmitt was seen to be losing coolant. Although Rupp turned immediately for France, with his engine rapidly overheating he faced either crash-landing in England or ditching in the Channel. He chose the former, carrying out a perfect belly-landing at RAF Manston, a favourite crash-landing location for JG 53.

Meanwhile, although Feldwebel Eduard Koslowski of 9. *Staffel* had shot down a Spitfire, the fighter flown by Oberleutnant Robert Magath of 7. *Staffel* was damaged in combat. He managed to limp home to France, however. Shortly thereafter the newly appointed *Staffelkapitän* of 8./JG 53, Oberleutnant Ernst-Günther Heinze, was forced to ditch his Bf 109E-7, although he suffered no injuries and was quickly rescued. Heinze, who had little combat experience, would have to wait until 14 May 1941 for the first of his 13 victories.

Having lost Walter Rupp, Oberleutnant Ignaz Prestele, *Staffelkapitän* of 2./JG 53, had also turned back early and the *Gruppe* was now being led by Oberleutnant Hans Ohly, as Hauptmann Hans-Karl Mayer had only just returned from leave. It is not known precisely why Mayer was not on this mission, although he was indeed airborne testing his new Bf 109E-7 for he heard over the radio the difficulties that the *Geschwader*, and particularly I. *Gruppe*, was experiencing. It is thought that he then tried to help, but exactly what happened next remains a mystery.

Pilots and groundcrew at Le Touquet on 9 November 1940. They are, from left to right, Leutnant Erich Schmidt, Hauptmann Wolf-Dietrich Wilcke, Hauptmann Heinz Bretnütz (back to camera), Oberleutnant Kurt Brändle (face obscured behind unidentified man in peaked hat), Hauptmann Hans-Heinrich Brustellin (with cigarette), Unteroffizier Heinrich Rühl (far back over Brustellin's left shoulder), Feldwebel Stefan Litjens, Major Günther Von Maltzahn (by car door) and Leutnant Siegfried Fischer (far right)

Hans Ohly's log book records that he took off at 1440 hrs British time and landed at 1600 hrs, and that on this mission Walter Rupp was shot down. Ohly makes no mention of the loss of Hans-Karl Mayer. RAF sources state that Rupp crash-landed at 1545 hrs, which tallies with German records. Just one claim was filed by I. *Gruppe*, Leutnant Wolfgang Tonne of 3./JG 53 downing a Spitfire south of London at 1537 hrs UK time for his fourth victory. Thus, it can be assumed that Mayer was lost between 1515 hrs and 1600 hrs UK time. It has been suggested that he was picked off by future ace Plt Off Edward 'Hawkeye' Wells of No 41 Sqn, but this unit intercepted a raid that was first reported at 1635 hrs, and Wells' claim was for a lone Bf 109 travelling south at 1715 hrs. If Mayer was indeed shot down, No 74 Sqn claimed to have destroyed three Bf 109s, with two more as probables, in the Maidstone-Gravesend area at around 1530 hrs, while No 222 Sqn claimed two Bf 109s destroyed and two damaged near Hornchurch, in Essex, at 1525 hrs.

In addition to those aircraft lost by JG 53, the Luftwaffe suffered just one more Bf 109 casualty that day when ace Oberleutnant Karl-Gottfried Nordmann, *Staffelkapitän* of 12./JG 51, force-landed his aircraft on the beach at Wissant after combat. Nordmann had made two claims on the 17th at 1655 hrs and 1657 hrs British time, so it appears he was involved in the later raid. It is therefore assumed that Mayer was shot down by either ace Flg Off Desmond McMullen or Sgt John Burgess, both from No 222 Sqn. The former's combat report, particularly the last sentence, makes interesting, and somewhat mystifying, reading;

'I was Yellow Leader at 24,000 ft. The squadron leader sighted a formation of Me 109s. I attacked the rearmost of four enemy aircraft slightly apart from the main formation. I opened fire at approximately 100 yards and closed in. Enemy aircraft became enveloped in black smoke and appeared to be out of control. About 10,000 ft, enemy aircraft straightened out and kept on diving, doing gentle turns. We went below cloud almost to sea level, where enemy aircraft dived into the sea. The camouflage was battleship grey with very prominent crosses. The pilot made no real attempt at evasive action and appeared to have had little more than the bare knowledge of how to fly.'

Ten days later a body was washed ashore at Littlestone, in Kent, and taken to the mortuary at RAF Hawkinge. It was that of a German airman, and carried no form of identification apart from the identity disc number 67005/1 – 67005 denoted 1./JG 53. A few weeks later RAF intelligence realised that they had buried Hans-Karl Mayer as an unknown German officer, and reported;

'The identity disc number 67005/1 is that of 1./JG 53, but this officer was *Gruppenkommandeur* of I./JG 53. He is thought to have been previously the *Staffelkapitän* of 1. *Staffel*, and this is no doubt where he got his identity disc. His position as *Staffelkapitän* is confirmed by the individual number 1 on the disc. From interrogation, it has been ascertained that he failed to return from a war flight about three weeks ago. The exact cause is not known. Hauptmann Mayer was a promising officer who had fought in Spain with the *Legion Condor* and had won several medals. In September last, when he claimed 20 victories, he was awarded the Knight's Cross.'

Mayer's loss must have been a shock not only to JG 53, but for the Luftwaffe. He was the first Luftwaffe *Ritterkreuz* winner to be killed in the war, albeit Hauptmann Horst Tietzen of 5./JG 51, another former *Legion Condor* pilot with seven victories in Spain, received the *Ritterkreuz* posthumously after he was shot down and killed on 18 August 1940, having destroyed 20 aircraft in World War 2. Command of I. *Gruppe* now passed to Hauptmann Hans-Heinrich Brustellin, who transferred from I./JG 51. For the rest of October, and indeed for the rest of the year up to 20 December, when the *Gruppe* moved back to Germany, there were no more victories and just two more combat losses. Both of the latter occurred on 2 December when Leutnant Wolfgang Fischer and Fähnrich Wolfgang Hauffe were shot down by No 74 Sqn while on a 'Freie Jagd'. Hauffe had only just joined 1. *Staffel* and had already been involved in an accident on 16 November. Wounded in the engagement, he was duly rescued from the sea and was eventually killed in action on 29 October 1944. The body of Fischer, who had only recently moved from 3. *Staffel* and had three confirmed victories to his name, was never recovered.

During the same period II. *Gruppe* was more successful than I. *Gruppe* in terms of aerial victories. Between 20 October and 30 November II./JG 53 shot down 22 aircraft and saw a number of its aces increase their scores. Amongst the latter was Hauptmann Heinz Bretnütz, whose fighter was damaged in combat on the day (20 October) he claimed his 20th victory. By the time JG 53 returned to Germany in December for rest and re-equipment, his score stood at 26, Stefan Litjens (4. *Staffel*) had six, Oberleutnant Kurt Brändle (5. *Staffel*) seven and Oberleutnant Gerhard Michalski (*Stab*. II./JG 53) eight.

As a direct result of it having seen more action in the late autumn of 1940, II. *Gruppe's* losses were higher than those of I. *Gruppe* – a total of 12 aircraft destroyed, with six pilots killed and four becoming PoWs. Among them there were three noteworthy losses. Oberfeldwebel Werner Kauffmann of 4. *Staffel*, who had gained his seventh, and last, victory on 5 October, had his aircraft damaged in combat, possibly with Flg Off Alec Ingle of No 605 Sqn, exactly three weeks later and ditched in the Channel at 1230 hrs. He was quickly rescued, none the worse for wear, by a Heinkel He 59 floatplane of *Seenotflugkommando* 3. On 11 November, almost to the hour, his was one of a number of German aircraft reported missing while escorting Stukas in the Thames Estuary. Then, on 1 December, former *Legion Condor* pilot Oberfeldwebel Bernhard Seufert was reported missing after combat with RAF fighters off Folkestone. The final noteworthy casualty occurred on 23 November when Feldwebel Josef Wurmheller of 5. *Staffel* ditched in the Channel after combat. His Messerschmitt had possibly been damaged in a duel with aces Flg Offs Alan Eckford or John Greenwood of No 253 Sqn, as the latter's combat report reveals;

'I was flying Red 4 with my squadron at 25,000 ft over Dungeness when I saw two aircraft some way below. I went to investigate but lost the aircraft on the way down, so I circled at 16,000 ft just off the coast, when two Me 109s passed in front and slightly above. I immediately turned behind them and from 200 yards fired two bursts of eight seconds and six seconds into [the] nearest machine. After the first three seconds I saw a cloud of white smoke emerge from the aircraft and it did a diving turn

One of a series of propaganda photographs purportedly taken to mark Oberfeldwebel Stefan Litjens scoring JG 53's 500th victory of the war on 15 November 1940 (although post-war records cast serious doubt on both total and date as given). This shot, taken on 20 November 1940, nevertheless shows a gathering of *Experten* who, between them, would add nearly 250 victories to the 'Ace of Spades" collective score. In the foreground, an ebullient 'Steff' Litjens (left), who had actually 'made ace' with two Spitfires confirmed on 11 November, receives a congratulatory handshake from Oberleutnant Franz Götz. To the rear (from left to right) are Oberleutnant Kurt Brändle, Hauptmann Heinz Bretnütz (partially obscured by Götz), Hauptmann Wolf-Dietrich Wilcke and Leutnant Erich Schmidt

down towards a large cloud mass in the Channel. I followed him, firing until the range was about 450 yards, and saw him dive almost vertically into the cloud at about 12,000 ft.'

Wounded, Wurmheller spent nearly five hours in the sea, his dinghy having been swept away, and he was not sufficiently recovered to return to operations until March 1941.

During the same period III. *Gruppe* claimed just four RAF fighters, two of which went to Leutnant Erich Schmidt, who was to end 1940 with 17 victories. Losses were correspondingly light – five fighters, with one pilot killed and two missing. On 23 November Leutnant Erich Schmidt's aircraft suffered very slight combat damage, but unlike Wurmheller, Schmidt managed to land back in France rather than ditch.

One of the last pilots from the *Geschwader* to be taken prisoner in 1940 was 22-year-old Oberleutnant Josef Volk of 9. *Staffel*. His career and fate is fairly typical of many of the 'Pik-As' pilots from that year. Volk joined II./JG 53 at the end of 1939 and moved to 9. *Staffel* in December. He gained his first victory during the Battle of France, a Potez 63 on the afternoon of 31 May, and his second, a LeO 451, nearly four hours later on the same day. At the end of the Battle of France he was posted to Vienna-Schwechat to be a 'Jagdlehrer' or fighter pilot instructor, but returned to 9. *Staffel* at the start of October 1940. In a month his war was over, as he recalled;

On 8 October 1940 Major Günther *Freiherr* von Maltzahn was appointed as *Kommodore* of JG 53, and on 20 November he ordered that the *Geschwader*'s famous 'Pik-As' badge be reapplied to the noses of his unit's Bf 109Es. Here, 'Henri' von Maltzahn (left) oversees the stencilling of the iconic 'Ace of Spades' onto his yellow-nosed 'Emil'. Having enjoyed considerable success leading II./JG 53 during the first year of the war (he was credited with ten victories between 30 September 1939 and 27 September 1940), von Maltzahn would claim a further 57 victories until he was promoted to Inspector of Fighters in Italy in early October 1943 (*John Weal*)

'I was shot down flying Yellow 12, as my Yellow 2 was being repaired. I remember it had the "Pik-As" badge on the cowling.'

Yellow 12 was one of the latest Bf 109E-8s, and what Volk has stated contradicts some of the contemporary records. Indeed, it was thought that following the *Geschwader*'s 500th victory (believed to have been claimed by Feldwebel Stefan Litjens on 11 November 1940) the *Geschwader* was officially given permission to wear the 'Pik-As' badge on the cowlings of its fighters on 20 November. However, during the morning of 11 November 9. *Staffel* was on a 'Freie Jagd', with Volk and Unteroffizier Robert Wolfgarten flying as the *Deckungsrotte*;

'On the return we were attacked by RAF fighters. I was hit in the engine and cockpit, and when the cockpit filled with flames I bailed out at 3000 m with a burnt parachute. I landed safely but was then threatened by farmers with pitchforks and other tools, and I had to defend myself with my flare pistol until I was taken prisoner by soldiers from a nearby training ground.'

Volk had been shot down by recently promoted Flt Lt Alec Ingle, who, as previously noted, had possibly been responsible for shooting down

Another photograph taken on 20 November, when JG 53 celebrated claiming its 500th aerial success and the return of the 'Pik-As' emblem to its Bf 109Es. These pilots are, from left to right, Leutnant Ernst-Albrecht Schulz (1./JG 53), Oberleutnant Kurt Brändle (*Staffelkapitän* 5./JG 53), Hauptmann Wolf-Dietrich Wilcke (*Gruppenkommandeur* III./JG 53), Major Günther von Maltzahn (*Geschwaderkommodore* JG 53), Hauptmann Heinz Bretnütz (*Gruppenkommandeur* II./JG 53), Oberfeldwebel Stefan Litjens (4./JG 53), Hauptmann Hans-Heinrich Brustellin (*Gruppenkommandeur* I./JG 53), Leutnant Erich Schmidt (*Stab.* III./JG 53) and Oberleutnant Franz Götz (*Staffelkapitän* 8./JG 53)

Oberfeldwebel Werner Kauffmann of 4./JG 53 on 26 October. Ingle's report leaves no doubt as to who he shot down;

'I saw two Me 109s appear in front of me, travelling west to east. I attacked the second one and in the ensuing dogfight, in which Blue 2 and 3 and Green 3 as well as a No 253 Sqn aircraft joined in, I got in two short deflection shots of about two seconds each. The evasive action taken consisted of diving, climbing, half-rolling and pulling out, at one time flying inverted for five seconds. Eventually one of the two aircraft involved led the enemy aircraft in my direction in a climb, from which he flattened out. I got directly astern during the climb and gave him an eight-nine second burst, closing from 200 to 50 yards. Large pieces of the aircraft broke off from the port wing root and the aircraft caught fire inside the cockpit. The pilot bailed out and landed four miles northeast of Rye at 0930 hrs.'

Sgt Albert Terry of the East Sussex Constabulary reported the following;

'At 0930 hrs an enemy 'plane Me 109 was shot down at Blackwall Bridge, Blackwall Marsh, Peasemarsh. The machine was buried deep in the ground and was a total wreck. The pilot bailed out and was captured at Stone near Wittesham. It is not known if he was injured or not. A guard was placed over the wreckage of the machine by 8th Battalion The Kings Liverpool Irish, stationed at Wittesham, Kent.'

Josef Volk eventually returned to Germany from Canada in February 1948. If it was any consolation to him, on 1 December 1940 Alec Ingle was shot down by Josef's former *Gruppenkommandeur*, Werner Mölders,

and his *Rottenflieger* Oberleutunant Hartmann Grasser, still with *Stab./JG 51*, as the No 605 Sqn diary records;

'As the squadron was returning for home at 15,000 ft near Maidstone it appears that the other upper 109 must have followed and shot down Flt Lt Ingle and Flg Off Passy, both of whom bailed out near Maidstone, each with a slight cannon wound in his calf.'

Both RAF pilots managed to bail out at 12,000 ft, Alec Ingle landing near the Ringlestone Inn at Harrietsham, while Cyril Passy came down near Hollingbourne. Ingle's wounds were more serious, and he was taken to a hospital at Leeds Castle.

Afterwards

In March 1941 JG 53 returned to northern France from Germany, the *Stab* arriving at St Omer Wizernes on or about the 15th, I. *Gruppe* reaching Crecy on 2 April, II. *Gruppe* flying into Arques on 13 March and III. *Gruppe* transferring to Berck on or about 30 March. There had been no changes made to the *Geschwader*'s leadership, but it was now flying the superior Bf 109F-1 and F-2.

The first victory of the year, and for the new fighter, went, unsurprisingly, to Hauptmann Heinz Bretnütz of II./JG 53 – a Spitfire north of Dungeness at 1720 hrs German time on 19 March, this claim matching perfectly with the loss of Sgt Arthur Eade of No 610 Sqn, who was bounced by a Bf 109 and, with shrapnel wounds in a shoulder and arm, force-landed at Thorneyfold Farm, in Bowdlestreet, at 1635 hrs UK time. However, the Bf 109F was not invulnerable. The first to come down on land was from *Stab./JG 3*, and it did so on 8 May. Just over 24 hours later a second example, flown by Leutnant Julius Heger of *Stab./JG 53*, crashed near Ashford, in Kent.

Leutnant Heger had joined *Stab./JG 53* in early March 1941, together with Oberfhanrich Franz Schiess. The latter would get his first victory over Russia on 22 June 1941, and by the time of his death on 2 September 1943 he had accounted for a further 66 aircraft and been awarded the *Ritterkreuz*.

A new arrival at Le Touquet in November 1940 was the Bf 109E-7, which now had the capability to carry a 300-litre auxiliary fuel tank on its centreline rack. Tank-equipped 'Emils' were used occasionally during *Jabo* escorts in the final weeks of 1940, although the E-7s were soon replaced by Bf 109Fs in the early spring of 1941

The *Stabsrotte* (two-aircraft element) of III./JG 53 taxies out at Le Touquet at the start of another mission in early December. The machine of *Gruppen* Adjutant Leutnant Erich Schmidt in the foreground carries 17 victory bars (he had claimed his final victory of the year on 30 November), while that of his *Kommandeur*, Hauptmann Wolf-Dietrich Wilcke, beyond displays 13. Schmidt's 'Emil' still wears the early style, narrow-bordered fuselage crosses that could be seen on many III. *Gruppe* aircraft right up until the end of 1940. Note too that although the 'Ace of Spades' is clearly in evidence again, neither machine has yet had its tailfin swastika restored

Heger recalled what it was like flying in the *Stab* alongside Major von Maltzahn, and perhaps explains why certain pilots were so successful;

'Both of us had no official function. We just had to fill up the *Geschwaderschwarm* of four 'planes. Our *Kommodore* had learned that there was no suitable place for him when flying in a big formation. He had to join the formation somewhere, and automatically took command of that smaller unit, in some way pushing the leader of that unit away. He hoped to gain more independence and more mobility by flying with his *Rotte* or *Schwarm*.'

Heger normally flew *Rottenflieger* to the *Geschwader* Adjutant, Hauptmann Hubert Kroeck, a former *Legion Condor* pilot and *Staffelkapitän* of 4./JG 53, while Schiess flew as *Rottenflieger* to Major von Maltzahn. However, on this occasion, Kroeck had just been posted and Heger was flying alongside Oberleutnant Wilfried Pufahl. The four pilots took off that evening (9 May) for a 'Freie Jagd' over Kent, not knowing that they were heading towards a patrol of four Spitfire VBs from No 92 Sqn. The RAF fighters were warned that there were six German aircraft near Folkestone and turned west, spotting and identifying them as Bf 109Fs. Heger related what happened next;

'We met four British fighters. Each side climbed to win the upper position but I had difficulties as my 'plane that day was not climbing as well as the others and I was hanging some distance behind. Two British 'planes dived away, obviously with the intention of luring us into a pursuit. One of them came close. I checked where the others were and reckoned to have a good chance of getting him. I had learned that the Bf 109F dived faster than the Spitfire, so I dived, but not at full power. However, instead of getting nearer, the distance increased. I opened fire from too far away, aiming with my tracer. He made evading movements and I had to handle the stick rather crudely to bring my tracers on to the target.

'Suddenly my 'plane began rocking terribly. I was pressed against the cockpit side and the roof alternately. This happened three or four times then my 'plane must have broken apart. Darkness was all around, and in my ears an infernal noise. My last thoughts before I lost consciousness was that the Lord forgive a young fellow of 21 – not a prayer but a curse. I cannot remember having pulled the handle of my parachute, but I must have, as when I regained consciousness I was hanging on my parachute and a British 'plane was circling me.'

Who shot Julius Heger down is hard to say with any degree of certainty. Ace Flg Off Trevor Wade saw a Bf 109 climbing to attack him from astern. He warned the others and then performed a violent series of manoeuvres, but his aircraft iced up and then went into a spiral dive to 15,000 ft, reaching a speed of 440 mph. When he managed to recover he could see that he had been hit in an ammunition drum and that he had a punctured glycol pipe. He had probably been attacked by von Maltzahn and Schiess, as the latter wrote in his diary;

'One Spit hangs a little below and we dive 500 m onto him. As the *Kommodore* closes to about 70 m the Spit rolls twice and dives vertically away. We go after him, but due to the great speed my elevators become almost inoperable. How I managed to pull out of that dive is still not clear to me.'

Meanwhile, Sgt Hugh Bowen-Morris had turned into the German aircraft, at which point he too saw a Bf 109 trying to get onto his tail. He took evasive action, diving to 10,000 ft. When a Bf 109 passed him he fired a short burst of 20 rounds from his cannon, but saw no result. However, Spitfire pilots of No 91 Sqn reported seeing a dogfight and a Bf 109 breaking up in the air.

Although already showing obvious signs of wear, this Bf 109F-2 (fitted with a telescopic sight mounted in the windscreen) assigned to Hauptmann Heinz Bretnütz, *Kommandeur* of II. *Gruppe*, can still arouse a certain amount of interest – or is that concern? – as it warms up at St Omer Arques in the spring of 1941. 'Pietsch' Bretnütz would claim five victories in the 'Friedrich' before JG 53 was posted east in preparation for Operation *Barbarossa* (*John Weal*)

1. *Staffel*'s Oberleutnant Hans Ohly dons an early pattern kapok life-jacket in preparation for another cross-Channel sortie in his brand new Bf 109F from Crécy in April 1941. Ohly was credited with three victories during the Battle of France, but his only claim during the Battle of Britain remained unconfirmed. He subsequently 'made ace' on the Eastern Front and survived the war with a score of 12 confirmed and three unconfirmed victories

Just the one claim was filed by Major von Maltzahn for a Spitfire off Calais (his last over the Channel Front), but as he had lost his *Rottenflieger* the claim was unconfirmed. In addition to the damage to Trevor Wade's Spitfire, Plt Off Bastian Maitland-Thompson crash-landed just outside the airfield at Biggin Hill and suffered cuts to his face and hands. However, over the Channel, the Spitfire of Sgt Bob Mercer of No 609 Sqn was damaged by a Bf 109. He attempted to get back but was killed when he crashed on the beach at St Margaret's Bay, in Kent.

The final word on the day's actions comes from Franz Schiess' diary;

'Our formation has been split up. Oberleutnant Pufahl returns alone. Shortly afterwards the *Kommodore* lands. He has shot down a Spitfire. Now we wait for Leutnant Heger. Why is he so long? Surely he doesn't want to carry out a singlehanded war over England. We stand on the airfield and smoke one cigarette after another and wait. The time passes slowly and we listen to the sound of every engine, but it is always another aircraft. The *Kommodore* looks at his watch. "Now he can have no fuel left," he says. The conversation is subdued and at dinner one chair is empty.'

By the time the *Geschwader* moved eastwards, on or about 8 June 1941, in preparation for Operation *Barbarossa*, the *Stab* had claimed four aircraft (all by the *Geschwaderkommodore*), I. *Gruppe* one aircraft, II. *Gruppe* 17 aircraft and III. *Gruppe* eight aircraft over France, the Channel and southern England during the previous three months. Major Günther von Maltzahn had now taken his total to 15 confirmed, while in II. *Gruppe* Hauptmann Heinz Bretnütz left for Russia with 31 victories, Feldwebel Josef Wurmheller had ten and Oberleutnant Gerhard Michalski nine. In III. *Gruppe*, Oberleutnant Heinz Altendorf now had seven victories and

Oberleutnant Franz Götz had ten. Only one new pilot achieved ace status before leaving for the Soviet Union. This was Leutnant Wolfgang Tonne of 3./JG 53, who claimed a Spitfire south of Boulogne at 1310 hrs German time on 26 April 1941 – this was possibly a Hurricane of No 56 Sqn flown by Plt Off Tom Guest, who was shot down and captured over France at around 1215 hrs UK time.

JG 53 was involved from day one, hour one of *Barbarossa*, with many of those 1940 aces scoring well on 22 June 1941, notably Major Günther von Maltzahn in the *Stab*, Oberleutnant Ignaz Prestele in I. *Gruppe*, Oberfeldwebel Stefan Litjens, Hauptmann Heinz Bretnütz, Feldwebel Josef Wurmheller and Oberleutnant Kurt Brändle in II. *Gruppe* and Hauptmann Wolf-Dietrich Wilcke, Oberleutnant Heinz Altendorf, Leutnant Erich Schmidt, Feldwebel Hermann Neuhoff, Leutnant Herbert Schramm and Oberleutnante Friedrich-Karl Müller and Franz Götz in III. *Gruppe*. However, despite the many victories, casualties began to rise. The first were Hauptmann Heinz Bretnütz, who on 27 June died of wounds received five days earlier while shooting down his 32nd aircraft, and Leutnant Erich Schmidt, who received the *Ritterkreuz* on 23 July, only to be reported missing on 31 August, possibly shot down by flak. He had been credited with 47 aircraft destroyed in little over a year. Many more 'Pik-As' pilots attained ace status in the remaining four years of the war, but few would survive into peacetime.

In this busy scene, probably taken at I./JG 53's St Omer Arques home in March-April 1941, mechanics can be seen working on the engines of a number of brand new Bf 109F-2s from both the *Stabsschwarm* and I. *Gruppe* (*EN-Archive*)

APPENDICES

Jagdgeschwader 53 Executive Officers in 1940

Geschwaderkommodore

Major/Oberstleutnant Hans-Jürgen von Cramon-Taubadel	30/9/40	To RLM
Major Günther von Maltzahn	9/10/40	From II./JG 53

I. *Gruppenkommandeur*

Hauptmann Lothar von Janson	30/6/40	To RLM
Hauptmann Albert Blumensaat	1/7/40 to 25/8/40	From IV.(N)/JG 2 to EGR Merseburg
Hauptmann Hans Karl Mayer	2/9/40 to 17/10/40(+)	From 1./JG 53
Hauptmann Hans-Heinrich Brustellin	10/40	From I./JG 51

1. *Staffelkapitän*

Hauptmann Hans-Karl Mayer	2/9/40	To I./JG 53
Oblt Hans Ohly	2/9/40	From 1./JG 53

2. *Staffelkapitän*

Hauptmann Rolf Pingel	5/6/40	To III./JG 53
Oberleutnant Ignaz Prestele (*Staffelführer*)	5/6/40 to 20/6/40	From 2./JG 53
Hauptmann Rolf Pingel	20/6/40 to 21/8/40	To I./JG 26
Oberleutnant Ignaz Prestele	21/8/40	From 2./JG 53

3. *Staffelkapitän*

Oberleutnant Wolfgang Lippert	3/9/40	To II./JG 27
Oberleutnant Julius Haase	4/9/40 to 15/9/40(+)	From 3./JG 53
Oberleutnant Walter Rupp	15/9/40 to 17/10/40(PoW)	From hospital
Oberleutnant Werner Ursinus	27/10/40	From *Stab.* II./JG 53

II. *Gruppenkommandeur*

Hauptmann Günther von Maltzahn	8/10/40	To *Stab.*/JG 53
Hauptmann Heinz Bretnütz	9/10/40	From 6./JG 53

4. *Staffelkapitän*

Oberleutnant Hubert Kroeck	8/40	To Erg St./JG 53
Oberleutnant Günther Schulze-Blanck	8/40 to 9/9/40(+)	From 4./JG 53
Oberleutnant Richard Vogel	9/9/40 to 10/10/40(+)	From 4./JG 53
Oberleutnant Kurt Liedke	10/40	From 5./JG 53

5. *Staffelkapitän*

Oberleutnant Rudolf Goy	10/9/40	To 1./JFS 5
Oberleutnant Kurt Brändle	9/40	From 4./JG 53

6. *Staffelkapitän*

Oberleutnant/Hauptmann Heinz Bretnütz	9/10/40	To II./JG 53
Oberleutnant Otto Böhner	9/10/40	From *Stab.* II./JG 53

III. *Gruppenkommandeur*

Hauptmann Werner Mölders	5/6/40(PoW)	To JG 51
Hauptmann Rolf Pingel (*Gruppenführer*)	5/6/40 to 20/6/40	From 2./JG 53 and to I./JG 26
Hauptmann Harro Harder	13/7/40 to 12/8/40(+)	From JFS 1
Hauptmann Wolf-Dietrich Wilcke	12/8/40	From 7./JG 53

7. *Staffelkapitän*

Hauptmann Wolf-Dietrich Wilcke	18/5/40(PoW)	
Leutnant Hans Riegel (*Staffelführer*)	18/5/40 to 6/40	From/to 7./JG 53

Hauptmann Wolf-Dietrich Wilcke	6-7/40 to 12/8/40	From PoW/to III./JG 53
Oberleutnant Hans Riegel	12/8/40 to 6/9/40(+)	From 7./JG 53
Leutnant/Oberleutnant Heinz Altendorf	6/9/40	From 7./JG 53

8. Staffelkapitän

Oberleutnant Hans von Hahn	20/8/40	To I./JG 3
Oberleutnant Heinz Kunert	20/8/40 to 8/9/40(+)	From 8./JG 53
Oberleutnant Walter Fiel	8/9/40 to 2/10/40(PoW)	From I./JG 3
Hauptmann Ernst-Günther Heinze	10/40	From 2./JFS 5

9. Staffelkapitän

Oberleutnant Ernst Boenigk	7/40	To JaFü 3
Oberleutnant Jakob Stoll	7/40 to 17/9/40(+)	From 9./JG 53
Oberleutnant Franz Götz	17/9/40	From 9./JG 53

Jagdgeschwader 53 pilots with five or more victories in 1940

Stab.

	STAFFEL	1940 VICTORIES	DECORATION(S)/FATE
Major Günther von Maltzahn	*Gruppenkommandeur* and *Geschwaderkommodore*	11	Awarded *Ritterkreuz* and survived war

I. Gruppe

Feldwebel Heinrich Höhnisch	1.	6	PoW 9/9/40
Hauptmann Wolfgang Lippert	*Staffelkapitän* 3.	11	Awarded *Ritterkreuz* and killed on 3/12/41 with II./JG 27
Hauptmann Hans-Karl Mayer	*Staffelkapitän* 1. and *Gruppenkommandeur*	22	Awarded *Ritterkreuz* and killed on 17/10/40
Hauptmann Rolf Pingel	*Staffelkapitän* 2. and *Gruppenkommandeur* III./JG 53	10	Awarded *Ritterkreuz* and PoW on 10/7/41
Oberleutnant Ignaz Prestele	*Staffelkapitän* 2.	8	Killed on 4/5/42 with I./JG 2
Leutnant Alfred Zeis	1.	5	PoW on 5/10/40
Oberfeldwebel Franz Kaiser	2.	5	PoW on 21/4/42

II. Gruppe

Feldwebel Albrecht Baun	6.	5	Killed on 25/8/40
Oberleutnant Kurt Brändle	4. and *Staffelkapitän* 5.	7	Awarded *Eisernes Kreuz* and killed on 3/11/43 with II./JG 3
Hauptmann Heinz Bretnütz	*Staffelkapitän* 6. and *Gruppenkommandeur* II./JG 53	26	Awarded *Ritterkreuz* and killed on 27/6/41
Oberfeldwebel Werner Kauffmann	4.	7	Killed on 11/11/40
Feldwebel Stefan Litjens	4.	6	Awarded *Ritterkreuz* and survived war
Oberleutnant Gerhard Michalski	*Stab.* II./JG 53	8	Awarded *Ritterkreuz* and survived war
Oberleutnant Günther Schulze-Blanck	*Staffelkapitän* 4.	6	Killed on 9/9/40
Unteroffizier Josef Wurmheller	5.	5	Awarded *Schwerten* and killed on 22/6/44 with III./JG 2

III. Gruppe

Oberleutnant Heinz Altendorf	*Staffelkapitän* 7.	6	PoW on 16 December 1941
Oberleutnant Georg Claus	*Stab.* III./JG 53	7	To 1./JG 51 and killed on 11/11/40
Feldwebel Hans Galubinski	7.	9	PoW 6/6/40 and later released, then killed with I./JG 101 on 13/1/44
Oberfeldwebel/Oberleutnant Franz Götz	9.	9	Awarded *Ritterkreuz* and survived war
Hauptmann Hans von Hahn	*Staffelkapitän* 7.	8	Awarded *Ritterkreuz* and survived war
Hauptmann Harro Harder	*Gruppenkommandeur* III./JG 53	6	Killed on 12/8/40
Oberleutnant Hans Kunert	*Staffelkapitän* 8.	9	Killed on 8/9/40
Hauptmann Werner Mölders	*Gruppenkommandeur* III./JG 53	25	PoW on 5/5/40 and released. Awarded *Brillianten* and killed on 22/11/41
Leutnant Friedrich-Karl Müller	8. and III./JG 53	10	Awarded *Eisernes Kreuz* and killed with JG 3 on 29/5/44
Feldwebel Hermann Neuhoff	7.	10	Awarded *Ritterkreuz* and PoW on 9/4/42

Leutnant Erich Schmidt	9.	17	Awarded *Ritterkreuz* and killed on 31/8/41
Feldwebel Herbert Schramm	7.	8	Awarded *Eisernes Kreuz* and killed on 1/12/43 with 5./JG 27
Unteroffizier Hans-Georg Schulte	7.	7	PoW on 6/9/40
Oberleutnant Jakob Stoll	*Staffelkapitän* 9.	13	Killed on 17/9/40
Hauptmann Wolf Dietrich Wilcke	*Staffelkapitän* 7. and *Gruppenkommandeur* III./JG 53	13	Awarded *Schwerten* and killed on 23/3/44 with JG 3

Jagdgeschwader 53 aces' claims in 1940

Stab.

DATE	STAFFEL	NAME	TYPE	VICTORY NUMBER	TIME	DETAILS
12/10/40	*Stab.*	Major Günther von Maltzahn	Hurricane	11	1740 hrs	
1/12/40	*Stab.*	Major Günther von Maltzahn	Hurricane	12	1515 hrs	

I. *Gruppe*

DATE	STAFFEL	NAME	TYPE	VICTORY NUMBER	TIME	DETAILS
7/4/40	3. *Staffel*	Oberleutnant Wolfgang Lippert	Spitfire	2	1250 hrs	Southwest Diedenhofen. Hurricane of No 73 Sqn. flown by Flg Off G Brotchie. Shot down over Thionville
21/4/40	1. *Staffel*	Oberleutnant Hans-Karl Mayer	Hurricane	2	1205 hrs	Northwest Merzig. Hurricane of No 73 Sqn flown by Plt Off P Walker. Force-landed northwest of Merzig
10/5/40	3. *Staffel*	Oberleutnant Wolfgang Lippert	Curtiss	3	1355 hrs	Southwest Metz. Possibly MB.152 (serial 545) of GC 2/8 that crashed at Jaulny. Capt A Astier killed
11/5/40	1. *Staffel*	Oberleutnant Hans-Karl Mayer	MS.406	3	0753 hrs	10–15 km South Metz. Possibly MS.406 (946) of GC 2/2 that crashed between Blénod-les-Toul and Ochey. Capt P Hyvernaud killed
14/5/40	2. *Staffel*	Hauptmann Rolf Pingel	Bloch 151	3	1120 hrs	South Sedan
14/5/40	2. *Staffel*	Hauptmann Rolf Pingel	Bloch 151	4	1122 hrs	South Sedan
14/5/40	1. *Staffel*	Oberleutnant Hans-Karl Mayer	Hurricane	4	1623 hrs	Sedan. Possibly Hurricane L1591 of No 3 Sqn. Crashed three miles northwest of Villers-Cernay. Sgt Dennis Allen killed
14/5/40	1. *Staffel*	Oberleutnant Hans-Karl Mayer	Battle	5	1624 hrs	Sedan. Possibly Battle P5232/JN-I of No 150 Sqn. Crashed near Raucourt-et-Flaba. Flt Sgt G Barker plus one killed, one injured
14/5/40	1. *Staffel*	Unteroffizier Heinrich Höhnisch	Hurricane	1	1625 hrs	Sedan. Possibly Hurricane L1908 of No 3 Sqn. Crashed near Annelles. Plt Off C Jefferies bailed out unwounded
14/5/40	2. *Staffel*	Feldwebel Franz Kaiser	Battle	2	1625 hrs	Sedan
14/5/40	1. *Staffel*	Oberleutnant Hans-Karl Mayer	Blenheim	6	1630 hrs	Sedan
14/5/40	1. *Staffel*	Unteroffizier Heinrich Höhnisch	Battle	2	1630 hrs	Southwest Sedan. Possibly Battle L5516/PM-O of No 103 Sqn. Crash-landed south of Sedan. Sgt G Beardlsey and LAC G F Lewis safe
14/5/40	2. *Staffel*	Hauptmann Rolf Pingel	Blenheim	5	1630 hrs	Sedan
14/5/40	1. *Staffel*	Unteroffizier Heinrich Höhnisch	Battle	3	1635 hrs	Southwest Sedan
14/5/40	1. *Staffel*	Oberleutnant Hans-Karl Mayer	Blenheim	7	1640 hrs	Southwest Sedan. Possibly Blenheim N6230 of No 114 Sqn. Crashed at La Casine. Flg Off H Newberry plus one crew injured, one killed
14/5/40	1. *Staffel*	Oberleutnant Hans-Karl Mayer	Battle	8	1655 hrs	South Sedan
14/5/40	2. *Staffel*	Oberleutnant Ignaz Prestele	Battle	4	1655 hrs	South Sedan. Possibly Battle L5232 of No 218 Sqn. Crashed at Sauville. Plt Off W A R Harris wounded, two killed
14/5/40	3. *Staffel*	Oberleutnant Wolfgang Lippert	Wellington	4	1930 hrs	Sedan. Possibly one of three Blenheims lost by No 21 Sqn
15/5/40	3. *Staffel*	Oberleutnant Wolfgang Lippert	Bloch 151	5	1613 hrs	South Charleville. Possibly MB.152 (189) of GC 3/1. Crashed at La Neuville-aux-Haies. Adjt R Autier killed
20/5/40	3. *Staffel*	Oberleutnant Wolfgang Lippert	Curtiss	6	1835 hrs	Noyon

25/5/40	1. Staffel	Oberleutnant Hans-Karl Mayer	Curtiss	9	1205 hrs	South Attigny. Two H-75s (121 and 220) of GC II/4 collided when attacked and crashed near Machault. Adjt P Villey and Sgt F Dietrich killed
26/5/40	2. Staffel	Hauptmann Rolf Pingel	Hurricane	6	1055 hrs	Hurricane TP-H of No 73 Sqn. Crashed at Chuffiliy-Roche. Plt Off F Sydenham killed
27/5/40	2. Staffel	Feldwebel Franz Kaiser	Potez 631	3	1916 hrs	West Noyon. Possibly Potez 631 (146) of ECN 4/13. Crash-landed at Chavigny. Adjt A Guichard killed, two safe
3/6/40	3. Staffel	Oberleutnant Wolfgang Lippert	Spitfire	7	1420 hrs	South Paris. Possibly MB.152 of GC II/1. Crashed Bretigny-sur-Orge. Sgt P Guitard wounded
3/6/40	1. Staffel	Leutnant Alfred Zeis	Curtiss	1	1445 hrs	Brie Comte Robert. Dewoitine D.520 (114) of GC I/3. Crashed at Faviéres. Sgt R Robert killed
9/6/40	3. Staffel	Oberleutnant Wolfgang Lippert	Curtiss	8	1450 hrs	Proult. Possibly H-75 (218) of GC II/4. Crashed between Roizy and Sault-Ste-Remy. Sous-Lt C Plubeau wounded
9/6/40	1. Staffel	Unteroffizier Heinrich Höhnisch	MS.406	4	1455 hrs	Northwest Reims. Possibly MB.152 (681) of GC II/6. Crashed on landing at Reims. Adj A Laguet wounded
12/8/40	1. Staffel	Hauptmann Hans-Karl Mayer	Hurricane	10	1320 hrs	
12/8/40	1. Staffel	Hauptmann Hans-Karl Mayer	Hurricane	11	1325 hrs	Channel. Hurricanes on 12 August believed to be No 145 Sqn aircraft flown by Plt Offs W Pankratz and J M Harrison and Sgt J Kwiecinski
13/8/40	1. Staffel	Hauptmann Hans-Karl Mayer	Hurricane	12	1700 hrs	Portland
13/8/40	1. Staffel	Unteroffizier Heinrich Höhnisch	Hurricane	5	1700 hrs	West Portland
13/8/40	1. Staffel	Unteroffizier Heinrich Höhnisch	Hurricane	6	1700 hrs	West Portland
15/8/40	1. Staffel	Hauptmann Hans-Karl Mayer	Hurricane	13	1845 hrs	Salisbury. Possibly Hurricane P3232 of No 601 Sqn. Shot down near Winchester. Plt Off G Cleaver wounded
15/8/40	2. Staffel	Hauptmann Rolf Pingel	Hurricane	9		
16/8/40	3. Staffel	Hauptmann Wolfgang Lippert	Spitfire	9	1800 hrs	
18/8/40	2. Staffel	Hauptmann Rolf Pingel	Spitfire	10	1532 hrs	
24/8/40	1. Staffel	Hauptmann Hans-Karl Mayer	Spitfire	14	1740 hrs	Isle of Wight. Probably Spitfire L1082/PR-A of No 609 Sqn. Returned to Middle Wallop badly damaged. Plt Off A Mamedoff uninjured
24/8/40	Stab. I	Leutnant Alfred Zeis	Spitfire	2	1740 hrs	Isle of Wight. Probably Spitfire N3239 of No 234 Sqn. Shot down over Isle of Wight and crashed at Merstone. Plt Off J Zurakowski uninjured
25/8/40	1. Staffel	Hauptmann Hans-Karl Mayer	Hurricane	15	1830 hrs	West Portland. Possibly Hurricane V7407 of No 17 Sqn. Flt Lt A Bayne bailed out unwounded
25/8/40	1. Staffel	Leutnant Alfred Zeis	Hurricane	3	1838 hrs	South Portland
26/8/40	1. Staffel	Hauptmann Hans-Karl Mayer	Spitfire	16	1430 hrs	East Portmouth
26/8/40	1. Staffel	Leutnant Albrecht Zeis	Spitfire	4	1730 hrs	Northeast Portsmouth
26/8/40	1. Staffel	Hauptmann Hans-Karl Mayer	Spitfire	17	1735 hrs	Portsmouth. Spitfire X4188 of No 602 Sqn. Shot down off Selsey Bill. Sgt C Babbage safe
26/8/40	3. Staffel	Hauptmann Wolfgang Lippert	Spitfire	10	1735 hrs	Portsmouth
2/9/40	3. Staffel	Hauptmann Wolfgang Lippert	Hurricane	11	0855 hrs	
6/9/40	Stab. I	Hauptmann Hans-Karl Mayer	Hurricane	18	1030 hrs	Northwest Dungeness
6/9/40	Stab. I	Hauptmann Hans-Karl Mayer	Hurricane	19	1800 hrs	
8/9/40	2. Staffel	Oberleutnant Ignaz Prestele	Hurricane	5	1325 hrs	
9/9/40	Stab. I	Hauptmann Hans-Karl Mayer	Hurricane	20	1905 hrs	
12/9/40	1. Staffel	Leutnant Alfred Zeis	Blenheim	5	1715 hrs	5 km north Le Havre. Combat with three Blenheims of No 235 Sqn and three of No 59 Sqn. No aircraft lost

15/9/40	Stab. I	Hauptmann Hans-Karl Mayer	Spitfire	21	1245 hrs	15 km south London
15/9/40	Stab. I	Hauptmann Hans-Karl Mayer	Spitfire	22	1310 hrs	Maidstone
15/9/40	2. Staffel	Oberleutnant Ignaz Prestele	Hurricane	6	1555 hrs	
19/9/40	2. Staffel	Oberfeldwebel Franz Kaiser	Blenheim	4	1725 hrs	Hastings. Possibly Blenheim T4025 of No 53 Sqn. Plt Off C F Tibbitts plus two missing
29/9/40	2. Staffel	Oberleutnant Ignaz Prestele	Hurricane	7	1725 hrs	South London
29/9/40	2. Staffel	Oberfeldwebel Franz Kaiser	Hurricane	5	1725 hrs	South London
29/9/40	2. Staffel	Oberleutnant Ignaz Prestele	Hurricane	8	1738 hrs	South London

II. *Gruppe*

31/3/40	4. Staffel	Unteroffizier Werner Kauffmann	MS.406	1	1550 hrs	Southwest Saargermünd. Possibly MS.406 (177) of GC III/7. Crash-landed Metz-Frescaty. Sgt R Morlot uninjured
31/3/40	Stab. II	Hauptmann Günther von Maltzahn	MS.406	2	1553 hrs	Southwest Saargermünd. Possibly MS.406 (971) of GC III/7. Crashed and burned at Grostenquin 1555 hrs. Adj R Chavet killed
31/3/40	6. Staffel	Oberleutnant Heinz Bretnütz	MS.406	3	1555 hrs	Southwest Saargermünd. Possibly MS.406 (811) of GC III/7. Abandoned over Grostenquin. Sous-Lt Y Rupied bailed out wounded
31/3/40	6. Staffel	Oberleutnant Heinz Bretnütz	MS.406	4	1557 hrs	Southwest Saargermünd. Possibly MS.406 (212) of GC III/7. Force-landed Morhange. Sous-Lt Renaud wounded
31/3/40	6. Staffel	Feldwebel Albrecht Baun	MS.406	2	1557 hrs	Southwest Saargermünd. Possibly MS.406 (176) of GC III/7. Abandoned north of Morhange. Sgt M L'Hopital-Navarre wounded
31/3/40	Stab. II	Leutnant Gerhard Michalski	MS.406	1	1600 hrs	Southwest Saargermünd. Possibly MS.406 (229) of GC III/7. Force-landed at Vitry-le-Françeois-Vauclerc. Lt B Dvorak wounded
31/3/40	6. Staffel	Oberleutnant Heinz Bretnütz	Wellington	5	2000 hrs	
7/4/40	4. Staffel	Feldwebel Stefan Litjens	MS.406	Unconfirmed	1230 hrs	West Saarbrücken. MS.406 of GC III/3. Crashed at Morhange. Capt A Richard killed
10/5/40	4. Staffel	Feldwebel Stefan Litjens	Curtiss	1	1525 hrs	Metz
12/5/40	6. Staffel	Oberleutnant Heinz Bretnütz	Potez 63	6	1200 hrs	Luxembourg. Potez 63 (444) of GR 2/22. Crash-landed south of Luxembourg. Capt Lainey and two crew captured
13/5/40	4. Staffel	Oberleutnant Kurt Brändle	MS.405	1	1205 hrs	South Sedan. Possibly H-75 (33) of GC I/5. Crashed near Harricourt. Lt A Vrana safe
21/5/40	6. Staffel	Oberleutnant Heinz Bretnütz	Potez 63	7	1114 hrs	East Montmédy. Potez 63 (630) of GAO 518. Crashed at Stenay. Lt Frantz plus one wounded, one killed
25/5/40	6. Staffel	Oberleutnant Heinz Bretnütz	MS.406	8	2002 hrs	
7/6/40	6. Staffel	Oberleutnant Heinz Bretnütz	Bloch 151	9	0705 hrs	East Compiègne. Possibly H-75 (213) of GC 3/4. Crashed at Morte-Fontaine. Capt R Guieu killed
7/6/40	4. Staffel	Feldwebel Werner Kauffmann	Bloch 151	2	1105 hrs	Roye
8/6/40	4. Staffel	Oberleutnant Günther Schulze-Blanck	Balloon	1	1055 hrs	
8/6/40	4. Staffel	Feldwebel Stefan Litjens	Potez 63	2	1100 hrs	Possibly Potez 63 (331) of GAO 517. Crash-landed Château-Thierry. Sous-Lt Battle plus two wounded
8/6/40	4. Staffel	Feldwebel Werner Kauffmann	Potez 63	3	1100 hrs	Possibly Potez 63 (284) of GAO 1/551. Crashed at Vaux-en-Dieulet. Lt J Rouig plus one wounded, one killed
8/8/40	Stab. II	Hauptmann Günther von Maltzahn	Spitfire	3	1705 hrs	15 km South Swanage
8/8/40	6. Staffel	Hauptmann Heinz Bretnütz	Spitfire	10	1715 hrs	South Swanage
11/8/40	4. Staffel	Oberleutnant Kurt Brändle	Spitfire	2	1145 hrs	West Portland
13/8/40	4. Staffel	Oberleutnant Günther Schulze-Blanck	Hurricane	2	1737 hrs	
13/8/40	4. Staffel	Feldwebel Stefan Litjens	Spitfire	3	1740 hrs	North Dorchester
15/8/40	6. Staffel	Hauptmann Heinz Bretnütz	Spitfire	11	1845 hrs	Southwest Portland

15/8/40	6. Staffel	Feldwebel Albrecht Baun	Spitfire	5	1846 hrs	Southwest Portland
15/8/40	6. Staffel	Leutnant Gerhard Michalski	Hurricane	2	1850 hrs	Southwest Portland
15/8/40	6. Staffel	Hauptmann Heinz Bretnütz	Hurricane	12	1902 hrs	15–20 km Southwest Portland
16/8/40	6. Staffel	Hauptmann Heinz Bretnütz	Hurricane	13	1436 hrs	
16/8/40	6. Staffel	Hauptmann Heinz Bretnütz	Hurricane	14	1437 hrs	Victories 13 and 14 were possibly Hurricane P3576/GN-A flown by Flt Lt J Nicolson (badly wounded) and P3616 flown by Plt Off M King (killed) of No 249 Sqn. Both crashed near Southampton, the former near Millbrook, the latter at Toothill. Hurricane P3870, flown by Sqn Ldr E B King, returned slightly damaged
16/8/40	Stab. II	Hauptmann Günther von Maltzahn	Spitfire	4	1810 hrs	
16/8/40	4. Staffel	Oberleutnant Kurt Brändle	Spitfire	3	1815 hrs	West-southwest Isle of Wight
16/8/40	4. Staffel	Feldwebel Werner Kauffmann	Hurricane	4	1820 hrs	
24/8/40	4. Staffel	Oberleutnant Günther Schulze-Blanck	Hurricane	3	1743 hrs	South Bournemouth
25/8/40	4. Staffel	Oberleutnant Günther Schulze-Blanck	Hurricane	4	1840 hrs	
29/8/40	4. Staffel	Oberleutnant Günther Schulze-Blanck	Hurricane	5	1708 hrs	
1/9/40	Stab. II	Hauptmann Günther von Maltzahn	Hurricane	5	1210 hrs	
5/9/40	Stab. II	Hauptmann Günther von Maltzahn	Hurricane	6	1605 hrs	
5/9/40	6. Staffel	Hauptmann Heinz Bretnütz	Hurricane	15	1605 hrs	Hawkinge
6/9/40	Stab. II	Hauptmann Günther von Maltzahn	Hurricane	7	1010 hrs	
6/9/40	4. Staffel	Oberleutnant Günther Schulze-Blanck	Hurricane	6	1012 hrs	
6/9/40	4. Staffel	Feldwebel Werner Kauffmann	Spitfire	5	1014 hrs	
6/9/40	6. Staffel	Hauptmann Heinz Bretnütz	Hurricane	16	1016 hrs	
11/9/40	4. Staffel	Oberleutnant Kurt Brändle	Spitfire	4	1740 hrs	
24/9/40	Stab. II	Hauptmann Günther von Maltzahn	Spitfire	8	0953 hrs	Southeast London
26/9/40	5. Staffel	Oberleutnant Kurt Brändle	Spitfire	5	1738 hrs	West Isle of Wight
27/9/40	Stab. II	Hauptmann Günther von Maltzahn	Spitfire	9	1019 hrs	
27/9/40	4. Staffel	Oberfeldwebel Werner Kauffmann	Hurricane	6	1020 hrs	
27/9/40	Stab. II	Hauptmann Günther von Maltzahn	Spitfire	10	1625 hrs	
28/9/40	5. Staffel	Unteroffizier Josef Wurmheller	Spitfire	2	1345 hrs	
30/9/40	5. Staffel	Unteroffizier Josef Wurmheller	Hurricane	3	1743 hrs	20 km north Portland
5/10/40	6. Staffel	Hauptmann Heinz Bretnütz	Hurricane	17	1240 hrs	Maidstone
5/10/40	4. Staffel	Oberfeldwebel Werner Kauffmann	Hurricane	7	1250 hrs	Maidstone
10/10/40	Stab. II	Oberleutnant Gerhard Michalski	Spitfire	3	1140 hrs	Folkestone
11/10/40	Stab. II	Hauptmann Heinz Bretnütz	Spitfire	18	0855 hrs	
11/10/40	Stab. II	Oberleutnant Gerhard Michalski	Spitfire	4	0855 hrs	
12/10/40	5. Staffel	Unteroffizier Josef Wurmheller	Spitfire	4	1215 hrs	60 km north Brest
12/10/40	Stab. II	Hauptmann Heinz Bretnütz	Spitfire	19	1733 hrs	
16/10/40	5. Staffel	Unteroffizier Josef Wurmheller	Blenheim	5	1520 hrs	North-northeast Ile d'Ouessant
20/10/40	Stab. II	Hauptmann Heinz Bretnütz	Hurricane	20	1625 hrs	
26/10/40	4. Staffel	Feldwebel Stefan Litjens	Spitfire	4	1130 hrs	Tonbridge

28/10/40	Stab. II	Oberleutnant Gerhard Michalski	Hurricane	5	1728 hrs	20 km south London
1/11/40	Stab. II	Oberleutnant Gerhard Michalski	Spitfire	6	1540 hrs	
8/11/40	Stab. II	Hauptmann Heinz Bretnütz	Hurricane	21	1103 hrs	20 km northeast Brighton
8/11/40	Stab. II	Hauptmann Heinz Bretnütz	Spitfire	22	1737 hrs	
11/11/40	5. Staffel	Oberleutnant Kurt Brändle	Spitfire	6	1307 hrs	
11/11/40	5. Staffel	Oberleutnant Kurt Brändle	Spitfire	7	1315 hrs	
11/11/40	Stab. II	Hauptmann Heinz Bretnütz	Hurricane	23	1315 hrs	
11/11/40	4. Staffel	Feldwebel Stefan Litjens	Spitfire	5		
11/11/40	4. Staffel	Feldwebel Stefan Litjens	Spitfire	6		
15/11/40	Stab. II	Hauptmann Heinz Bretnütz	Lysander	24	1410 hrs	Over Channel. Lysander R7079 of No 4 Sqn. Plt Off P T Empson and Sgt J E Gethin killed
24/11/40	Stab. II	Oberleutnant Gerhard Michalski	Hurricane	7	1650 hrs	Gravesend
30/11/40	Stab. II	Hauptmann Heinz Bretnütz	Hurricane	25	1523 hrs	Ashford
30/11/40	Stab. II	Hauptmann Heinz Bretnütz	Hurricane	26	1525 hrs	Ashford
30/11/40	Stab. II	Oberleutnant Gerhard Michalski	Hurricane	8	1526 hrs	Ashford

III. *Gruppe*

2/3/40	Stab. III	Hauptmann Werner Mölders	Hurricane	4	1215 hrs	South Bitsch. Possibly Hurricane L1808 of No 73 Sqn. Crash-landed near Metz airfield. Flg Off E Kain uninjured
2/3/40	7. Staffel	Unteroffizier Hermann Neuhoff	Hurricane	1	1220 hrs	South Diedenhofen. Possibly Hurricane L1958 of No 73 Sqn. Crashed at Brulange. Sgt D Sewell unhurt
2/3/40	7. Staffel	Oberleutnant Wolf-Dietrich Wilcke	Hurricane	Unconfirmed	?	South Bitsch
3/3/40	Stab. III	Hauptmann Werner Mölders	MS.406	5	1355 hrs	12 km southeast Diedenhofen. Possibly MS.406 of GC II/3. Force-landed at Toul. Cpl K Korber wounded
11/3/40	7. Staffel	Oberleutnant Wolf-Dietrich Wilcke	Potez	2	1745 hrs	6 km north-northeast Sierck. Potez 63.11 (22) of GR I/22. Crashed on landing at Metz-Frescaty. Lt Meitret wounded, remainder unhurt
25/3/40	7. Staffel	Oberleutnant Wolf-Dietrich Wilcke	MS.406	3	1455 hrs	Southwest Saarbrücken. MS.406 (756) of GC III/3. Crash-landed at Grostenquin. Adj M Marias wounded
26/3/40	Stab. III	Hauptmann Werner Mölders	MS.406	6	1500 hrs	Wolkenfeld. Hurricane L1766 of No 73 Sqn. Shot down over Ritzing. Flg Off E Kain wounded
2/4/40	Stab. III	Hauptmann Werner Mölders	Hurricane	7	1210 hrs	South Saargemünd. Hurricane N2326 of No 1 Sqn. Shot down over St Avold. Flg Off C Palmer unhurt
20/4/40	Stab. III	Hauptmann Werner Mölders	P-36	8	1154 hrs	7 km east Saargemünd. H-75 (136) of GC II/4. Crash-landed near Bliesbruck. Adj R Cruchant wounded
23/4/40	Stab. III	Hauptmann Werner Mölders	Hurricane	9	1114 hrs	South Diedenhofen. Hurricane P2576 of No 73 Sqn. Shot down over Thionville. Sgt C N S Campbell bailed out wounded
12/5/40	7. Staffel	Feldwebel Hans Galubinski	Potez 63	1	1910 hrs	South Metz
14/5/40	7. Staffel	Unteroffizier Hans-Georg Schulte	MS.406	1	1020 hrs	10 km west Sedan
14/5/40	7. Staffel	Unteroffizier Hermann Neuhoff	MS.406	2	1030 hrs	Sedan
14/5/40	7. Staffel	Oberfeldwebel Franz Götz	MS.406	Unconfirmed	1030 hrs	Sedan
14/5/40	7. Staffel	Feldwebel Herbert Schramm	MS.406	Unconfirmed	1030 hrs	Sedan
14/5/40	7. Staffel	Feldwebel Hans Galubinski	MS.406	Unconfirmed	1030 hrs	Sedan
14/5/40	Stab. III	Hauptmann Werner Mölders	Hurricane	10	1630 hrs	Sedan. Possibly Hurricane P2689 of No 73 Sqn that crashed north of Noirval. Sgt L Dibden killed
14/5/40	8. Staffel	Leutnant Heinz Kunert	Hurricane	1	1630 hrs	North Sedan
15/5/40	Stab. III	Oberleutnant Georg Claus	Hurricane	2	1000 hrs	Vouziers
15/5/40	Stab. III	Hauptmann Werner Mölders	Hurricane	11	1305 hrs	Charleville. Possibly Hurricane P2870 of No 607 Sqn. Shot down between Givet and Dinant. Sqn Ldr L Smith missing
18/5/40	7. Staffel	Oberfeldwebel Franz Götz	Curtiss	Unconfirmed	1636 hrs	West Laon

18/5/40	7. *Staffel*	Unteroffizier Hermann Neuhoff	Curtiss	Unconfirmed 3	1638 hrs	West Laon
18/5/40	7. *Staffel*	Feldwebel Hans Galubinski	Curtiss	Unconfirmed 3	1640 hrs	West Laon
20/5/40	*Stab.* III	Hauptmann Werner Mölders	Wellesley	13	1915 hrs	Compiègne
21/5/40	*Stab.* III	Hauptmann Werner Mölders	MS.406	14	1730 hrs	Southwest Compiègne. Possibly MS.406 (925) of GC III/6 that force-landed north of Chantilly. Capt M J Sulerzycki uninjured
21/5/40	*Stab.* III	Hauptmann Werner Mölders	MS.406	15	1750 hrs	Southwest Compiègne
21/5/40	7. *Staffel*	Feldwebel Hans Galubinski	Curtiss	4	1910 hrs	East Paris
21/5/40	8. *Staffel*	Oberleutnant Hans von Hahn	LeO 451	2	1910 hrs	Chalons
21/5/40	*Stab.* III	Hauptmann Werner Mölders	MS.406	16	1918 hrs	Southwest Compiègne
21/5/40	7. *Staffel*	Leutnant Heinz Altendorf	Curtiss	2	1925 hrs	Southwest Compiègne
21/5/40	7. *Staffel*	Unteroffizier Hans-Georg Schulte	Curtiss	Unconfirmed		Southwest Compiègne
21/5/40	8. *Staffel*	Oberleutnant Hans von Hahn	MS.406	Unconfirmed		East Paris
21/5/40	8. *Staffel*	Oberleutnant Hans von Hahn	Curtiss	Unconfirmed		East Paris
22/5/40	*Stab.* III]	Hauptmann Werner Mölders	Potez 63	17	1750 hrs	Southwest Mourmelon. Potez 63 (315) of GAO 1/514. Shot down and crashed between Isse and les Grandes Loges, southeast Reims. Sous-Lt J Jacquet plus two killed
24/5/40	8. *Staffel*	Leutnant Heinz Kunert	Curtiss	2	1815 hrs	
24/5/40	8. *Staffel*	Oberleutnant Hans von Hahn	Curtiss	3	1815 hrs	
25/5/40	*Stab.* III	Hauptmann Werner Mölders	MS.406	18	1855 hrs	Compègne Forest. Possibly D.520 (211) of GC II/3. Crashed between Villers-Agron-Aiguizy and Romigny. Sous-Lt A Mikulasek killed
25/5/40	*Stab.* III	Leutnant Georg Claus	MS.406	3	1855 hrs	Compègne Forest. Possibly D.520 of GC II/3. Returned to Betz-Bouillancy. Sous-Lt A Troyes wounded
27/5/40	8. *Staffel*	Leutnant Heinz Kunert	Curtiss	3	0910 hrs	Compiègne Forest. Possibly MB.152 (555) of GC 2/8. Crashed Le Quesnel. Cpl A Kralik killed
27/5/40	8. *Staffel*	Leutnant Friedrich-Karl Müller	Curtiss	1	0910 hrs	Compiègne Forest
27/5/40	*Stab.* III	Hauptmann Werner Mölders	Curtiss	19	0910 hrs	Compiègne Forest. Possibly MB.152 (236) of GC 2/8. Abandoned over Château Blin de Bourbon. Sous-Lt H de Castel wounded
27/5/40	*Stab.* III	Hauptmann Werner Mölders	Curtiss	20	0911 hrs	Compiègne Forest
27/5/40	7. *Staffel*	Oberfeldwebel Franz Götz	MS.406	1	1412 hrs	10 km south Creil
27/5/40	7. *Staffel*	Feldwebel Herbert Schramm	MS.406	1	1415 hrs	10 km south Creil
27/5/40	7. *Staffel*	Leutnant Heinz Altendorf	MS.406	3	1420 hrs	10 km south Creil
27/5/40	7. *Staffel*	Feldwebel Hans Galubinski	Curtiss	5	1420 hrs	South Creil
27/5/40	7. *Staffel*	Unteroffizier Hermann Neuhoff	Caudron 710	4	1425 hrs	South Creil
31/5/40	9. *Staffel*	Leutnant Jakob Stoll	MS.406	3	1847 hrs	15 km west Abbeville
31/5/40	9. *Staffel*	Leutnant Jakob Stoll	MS.406	4	1850 hrs	15 km west Abbeville
31/5/40	8. *Staffel*	Oberleutnant Hans von Hahn	Curtiss	4	1908 hrs	Abbeville
31/5/40	*Stab.* III	Hauptmann Werner Mölders	LeO 451	21	1955 hrs	30 km south Abbeville. Possibly LeO 451 (29) of GB 4/31. Crashed between Le Caule and Ste Beuve. Capt Irumbery de Salberry plus one uninjured, one wounded, one killed
31/5/40	*Stab.* III	Leutnant Georg Claus	LeO 451	4	1955 hrs	Abbeville. Possibly LeO 451 (73) of GB II/31. Shot down between Amiens and Abbeville. Sous-Lt Rappaport and one bailed out uninjured, two bailed out wounded

1/6/40	8. *Staffel*	Leutnant Heinz Kunert	Hurricane	4	2005 hrs	Northwest Reims. Possibly Hurricane of No 73 Sqn. Crashed at La Malmaison. Plt Off I Potts PoW
1/6/40	8. *Staffel*	Leutnant Heinz Kunert	Hurricane	5	2009 hrs	Northwest Reims
1/6/40	9. *Staffel*	Leutnant Jakob Stoll	Hurricane	Unconfirmed		Northwest Reims. Possibly Hurricane of No 73 Sqn that returned damaged. Plt Off D Scott uninjured
2/6/40	8. *Staffel*	Leutnant Heinz Kunert	Potez 63	5	1245 hrs	La Selve. Possibly Potez 63 (804) of GAO 1/589. Lt J Cheysson and one killed, one wounded
3/6/40	9. *Staffel*	Leutnant Jakob Stoll	Hurricane	5	0905 hrs	North Creil. Possibly Hurricane P2867 of No 501 Sqn. Pilot not recorded
3/6/40	7. *Staffel*	Feldwebel Hans Galubinski	MS.406	6	1030 hrs	Montdidier. Possibly MB.152 of GC I/8. Damaged in combat. Sgt Maurel wounded
3/6/40	7. *Staffel*	Unteroffizier Hermann Neuhoff	Curtiss	5	1035 hrs	West Creil. Possibly MB.152 (567) of GC I/8. Crashed on landing at Claye-Souilly. Sgt J Dekastello killed
3/6/40	7. *Staffel*	Leutnant Heinz Altendorf	Potez 63	4	1035 hrs	Gourney. Possibly Potez 63 (117) of ECN 1/13. Crashed north of Gournay-sur-Aisne. Sous-Lt S Biger and two killed
3/6/40	Stab. III	Hauptmann Werner Mölders	Curtiss	22	1430 hrs	Paris. Possibly MS.406 (693) of GC I/6. Crashed at Monthéty. Sgt S Popelka killed
3/6/40	8 *Staffel*	Oberleutnant Hans von Hahn	Hurricane	5	1435 hrs	Paris. Possibly MB.152 of GC I/8. Damaged in combat. Sous-Lt V Tanguy unhurt
3/6/40	Stab. III	Hauptmann Werner Mölders	Spitfire	23	1440 hrs	Southeast Paris. Possibly MS.406 (1022) of GC I/6. Shot down near Ozoir-la-Ferrière. Sgt Jost wounded
3/6/40	8. *Staffel*	Leutnant Friedrich-Karl Müller	Hurricane	2	1455 hrs	Paris
3/6/40	8. *Staffel*	Oberleutnant Hans von Hahn	MS.406	Unconfirmed	1455 hrs	Paris
4/6/40	8. *Staffel*	Unteroffizier Hans-Georg Schulte	Potez 63	2	1815 hrs	Ormoy-Villers. Potez 63 (620) of GR 2/35. Capt J Robert and one killed, one wounded
5/6/40	7. *Staffel*	Feldwebel Hans Galubinski	Hurricane	7	0750 hrs	Paris. Possibly Hurricane of No 73 Sqn. Returned damaged. Sqn Ldr J More unhurt
5/6/40	7. *Staffel*	Unteroffizier Hermann Neuhoff	Hurricane	6	0750 hrs	Poix. Possibly Hurricane of No 73 Sqn. Returned damaged. Flg Off E Kain unhurt
5/6/40	Stab. III	Leutnant Georg Claus	Bloch	5	1113 hrs	West Compiègne
5/6/40	Stab. III	Hauptmann Werner Mölders	Bloch	24	1120 hrs	West Compiègne
5/6/40	8. *Staffel*	Leutnant Heinz Kunert	Bloch 152	7	1120 hrs	West Compiègne
5/6/40	Stab. III	Hauptmann Werner Mölders	Potez 63	25	1123 hrs	Northwest Pont Ste Maxence. Potez 63 (250) of GAO 501. Crashed at Sarron. Sous-Lt M Benoist plus two killed
5/6/40	7. *Staffel*	Oberfeldwebel Franz Götz	Potez 63	2	1430 hrs	Possibly Potez 63 (592) of GAO 509. Crashed Thil Manneville. Sous-Lt H Guillerme and two killed
5/6/40	8. *Staffel*	Leutnant Friedrich-Karl Müller	MS.406	3	1820 hrs	Compiègne
6/6/40	7. *Staffel*	Feldwebel Hans Galubinski	MB.151	8	0950 hrs	Southeast Soissons. Possibly MB.152 (379) of GC II/1. Crashed near Acy. Sgt P Chenélot killed
6/6/40	7. *Staffel*	Oberfeldwebel Franz Götz	Bloch 151	3	0950 hrs	Southeast Soissons. Possibly MB.152 (621) of GC II/1. Crashed at Plessis-Paté. Sgt M Gaudon killed
6/6/40	7. *Staffel*	Feldwebel Hans Galubinski	Bloch 151	9	0952 hrs	Southeast Soissons
7/6/40	8. *Staffel*	Unteroffizier Hans-Georg Schulte	MS.406	3	1651 hrs	Compiègne
7/6/40	8. *Staffel*	Oberleutnant Hans von Hahn	MS.406	6	1653 hrs	Compiègne
7/6/40	8. *Staffel*	Leutnant Friedrich-Karl Müller	MS.406	5	1653 hrs	Compiègne
9/6/40	7. *Staffel*	Oberfeldwebel Franz Götz	Curtiss	4	1010 hrs	Rethel-Attigny. Possibly H-75 (206) of GC II/4. Shot down near Moronvilliers. Sous-Lt Blanc wounded
9/6/40	7. *Staffel*	Feldwebel Hermann Neuhoff	Curtiss	7	1015 hrs	Rethel-Attigny. Possibly H-75 (89) of GC II/4. Force-landed southeast Bouy. Adj J Paulhan wounded
10/6/40	8. *Staffel*	Leutnant Friedrich-Karl Müller	MS.406	6	0820 hrs	Southwest Reims
10/6/40	8. *Staffel*	Leutnant Friedrich-Karl Müller	MS.406	7	0830 hrs	Southwest Reims

Date	Unit	Pilot	Type	Claim	Time	Location/Notes
10/6/40	8. Staffel	Leutnant Friedrich-Karl Müller	MS.406	8	0830 hrs	Southwest Reims
11/6/40	7. Staffel	Oberfeldwebel Franz Götz	Bloch 152	5	1155 hrs	Reims. Possibly MB.152 (516) of GC I/6. Damaged in combat and crashed on landing near Crugny. Lt Pascal killed
11/6/40	Stab. III	Hauptmann Rolf Pingel	MS.406	7	1155 hrs	Reims-Epernay. Possibly MS.406 (821) of GC I/6. Shot down over Loivre. Capt Lefoyer captured wounded
11/6/40	7. Staffel	Feldwebel Hermann Neuhoff	Bloch 151	8	1203 hrs	Reims-Epernay. Possibly MB.152 of GC II/9. Force-landed at Chalons-en-Champagne. Sgt Daunizeau unhurt
11/6/40	Stab. III	Hauptmann Rolf Pingel	MS.406	8	1210 hrs	Southwest Epernay. Possibly D.520 (49) of GC I/6. Shot down near Epernay. Capt Guillaume de Rivals-Mazères wounded
11/6/40	Stab. III	Leutnant Georg Claus	MS.406	6	1210 hrs	Southwest. Possibly MS.406 (431) of GC I/6. Damaged in combat and crashed on landing. Sgt Standera injured
11/8/40	Stab. III	Hauptmann Harro Harder	Spitfire	2	1140 hrs	
11/8/40	Stab. III	Hauptmann Harro Harder	Spitfire	3	1150 hrs	20 km south Portland
11/8/40	Stab. III	Hauptmann Harro Harder	Spitfire	4	1153 hrs	Portland/Isle of Wight
12/8/40	9. Staffel	Leutnant Erich Schmidt	Spitfire	1	1237 hrs	East Isle of Wight
12/8/40	Stab. III	Hauptmann Harro Harder	Hurricane	Unconfirmed	1320 hrs	East Isle of Wight
12/8/40	Stab. III	Hauptmann Harro Harder	Hurricane	Unconfirmed	1325 hrs	East Isle of Wight
13/8/40	7. Staffel	Unteroffizier Hans-Georg Schulte	Blenheim	4	1150 hrs	Channel
15/8/40	Stab. III	Oberleutnant Georg Claus	Spitfire	7	2010 hrs	Théville. Spitfire N3277/AZ-H forced down intact. Plt Off R Hardy PoW
25/8/40	8. Staffel	Hauptmann Hans von Hahn	Spitfire	7	1827 hrs	10 km east Portland
25/8/40	8. Staffel	Oberleutnant Heinz Kunert	Spitfire	8	1829 hrs	10 km east Portland
25/8/40	9. Staffel	Oberleutnant Jakob Stoll	Spitfire	6	1836 hrs	10 km east Portland
31/8/40	Stab. III	Hauptmann Wolf-Dietrich Wilcke	Spitfire	4	2035 hrs	Dover
31/8/40	9. Staffel	Leutnant Erich Schmidt	Spitfire	2	2042 hrs	Dover
1/9/40	7. Staffel	Unteroffizier Hans-Georg Schulte	Hurricane	5	1220 hrs	Channel
1/9/40	Stab. III	Hauptmann Wolf-Dietrich Wilcke	Spitfire	5	1225 hrs	Channel
2/9/40	7. Staffel	Feldwebel Herbert Schramm	Spitfire	2	1750 hrs	Northeast Dungeness
5/9/40	7. Staffel	Unteroffizier Hans-Georg Schulte	Spitfire	6	1620 hrs	Thames Estuary
5/9/40	8. Staffel	Oberleutnant Heinz Kunert	Spitfire	9	1623 hrs	Thames Estuary
5/9/40	8. Staffel	Leutnant Friedrich-Karl Müller	Spitfire	9	1625 hrs	Thames Estuary
5/9/40	9. Staffel	Leutnant Erich Schmidt	Spitfire	3	1635 hrs	Thames Estuary
6/9/40	9. Staffel	Oberleutnant Jakob Stoll	Spitfire	7	1009 hrs	Thames Estuary
6/9/40	8. Staffel	Oberleutnant Friedrich-Karl Müller	Spitfire	10	1025 hrs	Dungeness
6/9/40	7. Staffel	Unteroffizier Hans-Georg Schulte	Spitfire	7	1910 hrs	Thames Estuary
8/9/40	9. Staffel	Oberleutnant Franz Götz	Hurricane	6	1335 hrs	Channel
8/9/40	7. Staffel	Leutnant Heinz Altendorf	Blenheim	5	1515 hrs	Channel
9/9/40	9. Staffel	Oberleutnant Jakob Stoll	Spitfire	8	1830 hrs	Northwest Calais
9/9/40	9. Staffel	Oberleutnant Jakob Stoll	Spitfire	9	1855 hrs	Northwest Calais
9/9/40	9. Staffel	Leutnant Erich Schmidt	Spitfire	4	1855 hrs	Northwest Calais
11/9/40	Stab. III	Hauptmann Wolf-Dietrich Wilcke	Albacore	6	1840 hrs	North Calais. 826 NAS suffered one ditched, three damaged
11/9/40	9. Staffel	Oberleutnant Jakob Stoll	Blenheim	10	1845 hrs	North Calais. No 235 Sqn lost two aircraft
15/9/40	9. Staffel	Leutnant Erich Schmidt	Spitfire	5	1244 hrs	Southeast London
15/9/40	9. Staffel	Oberleutnant Jakob Stoll	Spitfire	11	1245 hrs	Southeast London
15/9/40	7. Staffel	Feldwebel Herbert Schramm	Spitfire	3	1250 hrs	Southeast London

15/9/40	Stab. III	Hauptmann Wolf-Dietrich Wilcke	Spitfire	7	1300 hrs	Southeast London
15/9/40	9. Staffel	Oberleutnant Jakob Stoll	Spitfire	12	1303 hrs	Southeast London
15/9/40	9. Staffel	Leutnant Erich Schmidt	Spitfire	6	1308 hrs	10 km south London
15/9/40	Stab. III	Hauptmann Wolf Dietrich Wilcke	Spitfire	8	1515 hrs	Southeast London
15/9/40	9. Staffel	Oberleutnant Jakob Stoll	Spitfire	13	1533 hrs	Southeast London
15/9/40	9. Staffel	Leutnant Erich Schmidt	Spitfire	7	1536 hrs	Southeast London
15/9/40	9. Staffel	Oberleutnant Franz Götz	Hurricane	7	1540 hrs	Southeast London
15/9/40	7. Staffel	Feldwebel Hermann Neuhoff	Blenheim	9	1900 hrs	20 km northwest Etaples
17/9/40	9. Staffel	Leutnant Erich Schmidt	Spitfire	8	1641 hrs	Thames Estuary
17/9/40	Stab. III	Hauptmann Wolf-Dietrich Wilcke	Hurricane	9	1650 hrs	Thames Estuary
18/9/40	7. Staffel	Feldwebel Hermann Neuhoff	Spitfire	10	1055 hrs	Ashford
18/9/40	9. Staffel	Oberleutnant Franz Götz	Spitfire	8	2050 hrs	Thames Estuary
20/9/40	Stab. III	Hauptmann Wolf-Dietrich Wilcke	Hurricane	10	1240 hrs	Northwest Dungeness
20/9/40	7. Staffel	Leutnant Heinz Altendorf	Spitfire	6	1250 hrs	Northwest Dungeness
26/9/40	7. Staffel	Feldwebel Herbert Schramm	Hampden	4	1316 hrs	Possibly Blenheim R3809 of No 114 Sqn. Missing from operation to Boulogne. Sgt F Wheeler plus two missing
27/9/40	9. Staffel	Leutnant Erich Schmidt	Spitfire	9	1333 hrs	Thames Estuary
30/9/40	Stab. III	Hauptmann Wolf-Dietrich Wilcke	Spitfire	11	1158 hrs	15 km South Dungeness
30/9/40	Stab. III	Leutnant Erich Schmidt	Spitfire	10	1433 hrs	London
30/9/40	7. Staffel	Feldwebel Herbert Schramm	Spitfire	5	1438 hrs	London
30/9/40	Stab. III	Hauptmann Wolf-Dietrich Wilcke	Spitfire	12	1455 hrs	Dungeness/Hastings
30/9/40	7. Staffel	Feldwebel Herbert Schramm	Spitfire	6	1455 hrs	Dungeness/Hastings
30/9/40	9. Staffel	Oberleutnant Franz Götz	Spitfire	9	1510 hrs	Hastings
2/10/40	9. Staffel	Leutnant Erich Schmidt	Spitfire	11	1106 hrs	Thames Estuary
2/10/40	9. Staffel	Leutnant Erich Schmidt	Spitfire	12	1110 hrs	Thames Estuary. Probably Spitfire P9553 of No 603 Sqn. Plt Off P Dexter bailed out wounded
5/10/40	9. Staffel	Leutnant Erich Schmidt	Hurricane	13	1233 hrs	Thames Estuary
5/10/40	7. Staffel	Feldwebel Herbert Schramm	Hurricane	7	1840 hrs	Channel
7/10/40	9. Staffel	Leutnant Erich Schmidt	Spitfire	14	1420 hrs	Mayfield
10/10/40	9. Staffel	Leutnant Erich Schmidt	Spitfire	15	1130 hrs	Thames Estuary
10/10/40	Stab. III	Hauptmann Wolf-Dietrich Wilcke	Spitfire	13	1140 hrs	Thames Estuary
17/10/40	7. Staffel	Feldwebel Herbert Schramm	Spitfire	8	1100 hrs	Dungeness
1/11/40	9. Staffel	Leutnant Erich Schmidt	Spitfire	16	1245 hrs	Tunbridge Wells
30/11/40	9. Staffel	Leutnant Erich Schmidt	Spitfire	17	1130 hrs	North Dover

Jagdgeschwader 53 aces 1940 – Aircraft and personnel casualities

DATE	AIRCRAFT	UNIT	PILOT	DETAILS
15/5/40	Bf 109E-3 Wk-Nr 1347	Stab. II./JG 53	Hauptmann Günther von Maltzahn (Gruppenkommandeur)	Technical undercarriage problems – crash-landed Dockendorf. 70 per cent damage
18/5/40	Bf 109E-3	7./JG 53	Oberleutnant Wolf-Dietrich Wilcke (Staffelkapitän) PoW	Believed shot down by Sous-Lt Camille Plubeau of GC II/4 in combat west of Rethel, 1615 hrs. Pilot later released
20/5/40	Bf 109E-4 Wk-Nr 5010	Stab. II./JG 53	Hauptmann Günther von Maltzahn (Gruppenkommandeur)	Damaged in combat south of Sedan
26/5/40	Bf 109E-3	5./JG 53	Oberleutnant Kurt Brändle injured	Collided with Do 17 on the ground, Charleville. Written off

5/6/40	Bf 109E-4 <<+I	Stab. III./JG 53	Hauptmann Werner Mölders (Gruppenkommandeur) PoW	Shot down by Sous-Lt René Pomier Layrargues of GC II/7 in combat west of Compiègne and crashed at Ferme du Villersau, Canly, 1715 hrs. Pilot later released
6/6/40	Bf 109E-1	7./JG 53	Feldwebel Hans Galubinski PoW	Shot down by Adj Jean Crocq of GC II/1 southeast of Soissons and crashed north of Belleu 0850 hrs. Pilot later released
12/8/40	Bf 109E-4 'White 8'	1./JG 53	Hauptmann Hans-Karl Mayer (Staffelkapitän)	Damaged in combat off Isle of Wight with No 145 Sqn
12/8/40	Bf 109E-4 <<+I	Stab. III./JG 53	Hauptmann Harro Harder (Gruppenkommandeur) Missing	Missing from combat off Isle of Wight, 1325 hrs
12/8/40	Bf 109E-4	Stab. III./JG 53	Hauptmann Wolf-Dietrich Wilcke (Gruppen Führer)	Suffered engine failure on air-sea rescue mission late afternoon and ditched south of Portland. Pilot rescued overnight
13/8/40	Bf 109E-4 Wk-Nr 1508 'White 5'	1./JG 53	Unteroffizier Heinrich Höhnisch	Damaged in combat off Isle of Wight, 1700 hrs
25/8/40	Bf 109E-4	6./JG 53	Oberfeldwebel Albrecht Baun Missing	Missing from combat southwest of Portland 1845 hrs
6/9/40	Bf 109E-4 Wk-Nr 3751	4./JG 53	Oberleutnant Günther Schulze-Blanck (Staffelkapitän) Wounded	Hit in the cockpit in combat east of Tonbridge, Kent. 30 per cent damage
6/9/40	Bf 109E-4 Wk-Nr 1506 'White 5+I'	7./JG 53	Unteroffizier Hans-Georg Schulte PoW	Damaged in combat with either Sgt Edward Darling of No 41 Sqn, Sgt Ian Hutchinson or Plt Off Tim Vigors of No 222 Sqn and force-landed at Vincent's Farm, Manston, Kent, 1830–1850 hrs
8/9/40	Bf 109E-4 Wk-Nr 1171	8./JG 53	Oberleutnant Hans Kunert (Staffelkapitän) Killed	Collided with Bf 109E-1 Wk-Nr 3478 of Stab. I./JG 53 flown by Oberleutnant Heinz Wittmeyer (Gruppen Adjutant) off Cap Gris Nez
9/9/40	Bf 109E-4 Wk-Nr 1508 'White 5'	1./JG 53	Feldwebel Heinrich Höhnisch PoW	Probably shot down by Flt Lt Wilf Clouston of No 19 Sqn and crashed at Cherry Lodge Farm, Old Jail Lane, Biggin Hill, Kent, 1800 hrs
9/9/40	Bf 109E-4 Wk-Nr 0963	4./JG 53	Oberleutnant Günther Schulze-Blanck (Staffelkapitän) Killed	Crashed into Channel south of Hastings
12/9/40	Bf 109E	1./JG 53	Leutnant Alfred Zeis	Damaged in combat with Blenheim of No 235 Sqn, landed Octeville 1615 hrs
15/9/40	Bf 109E-4 Wk-Nr 5251	Stab. III./JG 53	Oberleutnant Friedrich-Karl Müller	Ran out of fuel and ditched in Channel. Pilot rescued
17/9/40	Bf 109E-4 Wk-Nr 5241	9./JG 53	Oberleutnant Jakob Stoll (Staffelkapitän) Missing	Missing from combat over Thames Estuary, 1650 hrs
20/9/40	Bf 109E-1 Wk-Nr 5175 'White 12+I'	7./JG 53	Leutnant Heinz Altendorf (Staffelkapitän)	Force-landed at Boulogne after combat. Five per cent damage
30/9/40	Bf 109E-1 Wk-Nr 6239	5./JG 53	Unteroffizier Josef Wurmheller	Crashed into Channel after combat. Pilot rescued
5/10/40	Bf 109E-4 Wk-Nr 1564 'White 3'	1./JG 53	Leutnant Alfred Zeis PoW	Probably shot down by Flg Off Paul Pitcher, No 1 Sqn RCAF and crashed at Sheerlands Farm, Pluckley, Kent, 1140 hrs
5/10/40	Bf 109E-4 Wk-Nr 5372	7./JG 53	Oberleutnant Heinz Altendorf (Staffelkapitän)	Force-landed at Cap Gris Nez after combat
17/10/40	Bf 109E-7 Wk-Nr 4138 '<<+'	Stab. I./JG 53	Hauptmann Hans-Karl Mayer (Gruppenkommandeur) killed	Believed shot down by No 222 Sqn into the Channel 1715 hrs
20/10/40	Bf 109E-7 Wk-Nr 4112 '<<+-'	Stab. II/JG 53	Hauptmann Heinz Bretnütz (Gruppenkommandeur)	Force-landed St Inglevert after combat. Five per cent damage
26/10/40	Bf 109E-1 Wk-Nr 6180	4./JG 53	Oberfeldwebel Werner Kauffmann	Possibly damaged in combat with Flg Off Alec Ingle of No 605 Sqn and crashed in Channel 1230hrs. Pilot rescued uninjured by He 59 of Seenotflugkommando 3
11/11/40	Bf 109E-4 Wk-Nr 0865 'White 9'	4./JG 53	Oberfeldwebel Werner Kauffmann Missing	Missing from combat over the Thames Estuary, 1315 hrs
23/11/40	Bf 109E-4 Wk-Nr 5212	5./JG 53	Feldwebel Josef Wurmheller Injured	Probably damaged in combat with Flg Off John Greenwood of No 253 Sqn and crashed in Channel off Berck-sur-Mer, 1710 hrs. Pilot rescued
23/11/40	Bf 109E	9./JG 53	Leutnant Erich Schmidt	Damaged in combat

COLOUR PLATES

1

Bf 109E-4 'White 8' of Hauptmann Hans-Karl Mayer, *Gruppenkommandeur* I./JG 53, Etaples, late September 1940

When Hans-Karl Mayer, *Staffelkapitän* of 1./JG 53, assumed command of I. *Gruppe* from Hauptmann Albert Blumensaat at the start of September 1940 he took his personal Bf 109E-4 with him. The rudder of the aeroplane shows 29 victories, this tally including eight barrage balloons – Mayer claimed his 21st and 22nd victories on 15 September. An early *Ritterkreuz*-holder, Mayer went on leave shortly after his 22nd victory, returning in mid-October 1940 and being killed in action on the 17th of that same month.

2

Bf 109E-4 Wk-Nr 1564 'White 3' of Leutnant Alfred Zeis, 1./JG 53, Le Touquet, October 1940

The rudder of Zeis' aircraft shows ten victory markings. He shot down his fifth, and last, aircraft (a Blenheim) on 12 September 1940, so the rudder shows a mix of aeroplanes and balloons that he claimed. Zeis was shot down and taken prisoner on 5 October 1940, this aircraft crashing at Sheerlands Farm in Pluckley, Kent.

3

Bf 109E-4 Wk-Nr 1508 'White 5' of Unteroffizier Heinrich Höhnisch, 1./JG 53, Rennes, August 1940

Höhnisch shot down four aircraft in the Battle of France but only managed two more in the Battle of Britain, both on 13 August 1940. During the latter combat his aircraft was slightly damaged by an RAF fighter. On 9 September Höhnisch, by now promoted to feldwebel, was shot down and taken prisoner – he had suffered burns by the time he bailed out. His aeroplane duly crashed at Cherry Tree Farm near the Old Jail Inn in Biggin Hill. The RAF noted the red band around the cowling (not mentioning that the cowling itself was yellow), and that on the underside of one of the wings were two penny-sized patches covering bullet holes marked by RAF roundels and the date 13.8.40. It is possible that the aircraft also carried six victory markings on the rudder.

4

Bf 109E-4 'Red 1' of Hauptmann Rolf Pingel, *Staffelkapitän* 2./JG 53, Cherbourg-Ost, August 1940

Legion Condor ace Rolf Pingel, *Staffelkapitän* of 2./JG 53, claimed his first victory of the Battle of Britain on 15 August (his ninth success overall), and gained his tenth three days later – both were probably achieved in this aeroplane. On 21 August he was posted to command I./JG 26. Pingel was awarded the *Ritterkreuz* on 14 September and was eventually shot down and taken prisoner on 10 July 1941, having by then claimed 21 aircraft in World War 2.

5

Bf 109E-4 'Black 2' of Oberleutnant Ignaz Prestele, *Staffelkapitän* 2./JG 53, Le Touquet, October 1940

Ignaz Prestele took over command of 2. *Staffel* from Hauptmann Rolf Pingel on the latter's departure on 21 August 1940. Prestele was another *Legion Condor* pilot who, by the start of the Battle of Britain, had been promoted from oberfeldwebel to oberleutnant. He achieved his third victory of World War 2 (having previously claimed four in Spain) on 8 September 1940, and he had taken his tally to six by the end of the month. Photographs from the period show him in the cockpit of this Bf 109, which had eight victory bars on its rudder. I. *Gruppe* moved to Le Touquet from Etaples at the start of October 1940. Prestele was subsequently promoted to hauptmann and posted to command I./JG 2. He was killed in action on 4 May 1942.

6

Bf 109E-4 'Red 14' of *Oberfeldwebel* Franz Kaiser, 2./JG 53, Neuville, September 1940

Curiously, 2. *Staffel* aircraft sported a mix of red and black numerals during 1940. Oberfeldwebel Franz Kaiser claimed his first victory of the Battle of Britain (a Blenheim, which was his fourth success overall) on 19 September 1940, and achieved his fifth and last of the campaign ten days later. He was captured on 22 April 1942 after his Bf 109F-4 suffered an engine failure following combat with a No 126 Sqn Spitfire, Kaiser ditching ten kilometres south of Marsa Scirocco, on Malta. By then he had a total of nine victories.

7

Bf 109E-4 'Yellow 1' of Oberleutnant Wolfgang Lippert, *Staffelkapitän* 3./JG 53, Darmstadt-Griesheim, spring 1940

This aircraft is believed to be the one used by *Legion Condor* ace Wolfgang Lippert, *Staffelkapitän* of 3. *Staffel*. By the start of the Battle of France he had shot down two aircraft, and it is possible that victory tally markings for these would have adorned the rudder of this aircraft. Having claimed nine French and British aircraft by the time he became *Gruppenkommandeur* of II./JG 27 at the start of September 1940, Lippert was awarded the *Ritterkreuz* on the 24th of that same month. He was eventually shot down on 23 November 1941 by a No 250 Sqn Tomahawk flown by high-scoring Australian ace Flt Lt Clive Caldwell, Lippert dying of his wounds in a Cairo hospital ten days later. His World War 2 tally had reached 30 victories by the time of his death.

8

Bf 109E-4 Wk-Nr 1325 'Yellow 13' of Feldwebel Walter Scholz, 3./JG 53, Etaples, 30 September 1940

Despite this aeroplane bearing four victory bars on the rudder, only one pf these was credited to its pilot, Feldwebel Walter Scholz – a Spitfire at 1550 hrs on 15 September 1940 – so it is possible that he was flying another 'almost' ace's aircraft when he was shot down in 'Yellow 13' and taken prisoner on 30 September. Although Scholz claimed when interrogated that he had force-landed due to a lack of fuel, a number of 0.303-calibre strikes were found in the aircraft's cooling system when it was examined by RAF Air Intelligence personnel in the field it had come down in in Langney, near Eastbourne in Sussex.

9
Bf 109E-4 <<+- of Hauptmann Günther von Maltzahn, *Gruppenkommandeur* of II./JG 53, Dinan, August 1940

Günther von Maltzahn was the first 'Pik-As' pilot to claim a victory in the Battle of Britain (his third of the war) when he shot down a Spitfire 15 km south of Swanage at 1705 hrs on 8 August. On 8 October he was promoted to command the *Geschwader*, by which time he had claimed ten aircraft destroyed – von Maltzahn had shot down another two before the end of 1940. A popular officer and trusted fighter pilot, von Maltzahn was awarded the *Ritterkreuz* on 30 December 1940 and the *Eichenlaub* on 24 July 1941. He survived the war, having claimed 68 aircraft destroyed.

10
Bf 109E-7 Wk-Nr 4112 <<+- of Hauptmann Heinz Bretnütz, *Gruppenkommandeur* II./JG 53, St Inglevert, 20 October 1940

Legion Condor veteran Heinz Bretnütz was the most successful 'Pik-As' pilot of 1940, shooting down 26 aircraft, firstly as *Staffelkapitän* of 6./JG 53 and then as *Gruppenkommandeur* from 9 October. On 20 October he shot down his 20th aircraft of the war while flying this machine – which suffered five per cent combat damage – and was consequently awarded the *Ritterkreuz* two days later. On 22 June 1941 Bretnütz was badly wounded while shooting down a Soviet bomber for his 31st victory of World War 2, and he died in hospital five days later.

11
Bf 109E-4 Wk-Nr 1244 'White 5' of Feldwebel Stefan Litjens, 4./JG 53, Mannheim-Sandhofen, spring 1940

Stefan Litjens had an unconfirmed victory on 7 April 1940, and by the end of the Battle of France he had two confirmed successes to his name. His first victory of the Battle of Britain came on 13 August, and by the end of the year his tally had risen to six, the last two being two Spitfires on 11 November. On 23 March 1944 Litjens lost an eye while attacking USAAF B-17s (he was credited with one confirmed destroyed and one unconfirmed), which ended his operational flying. Litjens had been awarded the *Ritterkreuz* on 21 June 1943, and had 32 confirmed and six unconfirmed victories to his name by the time he was wounded.

12
Bf 109E-4 Wk-Nr 0865 'White 9' of Oberfeldwebel Werner Kauffmann, 4./JG 53, Berck-sur-Mer, November 1940

Werner Kauffmann had been credited with three victories prior to the Battle of Britain, and his first of the latter campaign came on

16 August. On 26 October his fighter was damaged in combat, probably with Flg Off Alec Ingle of Hurricane-equipped No 605 Sqn, and he ditched Bf 109E-1 Wk-Nr 6180 in the Channel and was rescued without incident or apparent injury by an He 59 of *Seenotflukommando* 3. By then Kauffmann had shot down seven aircraft, and he had failed to add to his tally by the time he was killed in 'White 9' on 11 November 1940 when shot down into the Thames Estuary by RAF fighters while escorting Stukas from StG 1.

13
Bf 109E-3 'Yellow 11' of Oberleutnant Heinz Bretnütz, *Staffelkapitän* 6./JG 53, Mannheim-Sandhofen, March 1940

Heinz Bretnütz was not only the first *Staffelkapitän* of 6. *Staffel*, he was also the first pilot from II. *Gruppe* to claim a victory – a barrage balloon at 0955 hrs on 20 September 1939. His first success over an aircraft came on 25 September 1939, and by the start of the Battle of France his total stood at five. Photographs of this aircraft, which was assigned to Bretnütz during the 'Phoney War' period, show no victory markings.

14
Bf 109E-4 <<+I of Hauptmann Werner Mölders, *Gruppenkommandeur* III./JG 53, La Selve, May 1940

Werner Mölders shot down his 18th aircraft on 25 May 1940 and the next two 48 hours later, for which he was awarded the *Ritterkreuz*. This was probably the aircraft he was flying from La Selve when he was shot down by Sous-Lt René Pomier Layrargues in a D.520 of GC II/7 west of Compiègne on 5 June, by which time his tally of 25 victories in World War 2 made him the second most successful 'Pik-As' pilot of 1940.

15
Bf 109E-4 <<+I of Hauptmann Wolf-Dietrich Wilcke, *Gruppenkommandeur* III./JG 53, Le Touquet, September 1940

Originally commanding 7. *Staffel*, 'Furst' Wilcke had a slow and unlucky start to the war, being shot down and taken prisoner on 18 May 1940 without having added to his two confirmed and two unconfirmed victories from the 'Phoney War'. He returned to 7. *Staffel* upon the fall of France, and following the death of new III./JG 53 *Gruppenkommandeur* Hauptmann Harro Harder on 12 August 1940, Wilcke was temporarily leading the *Gruppe* when he was forced to ditch that same afternoon after his fighter suffered engine failure. Rescued several hours later, Wilke was duly confirmed as *Gruppenkommandeur*, but he had to wait until 31 August for his third victory of the war. By the end of September his tally stood at 11, but he gained only one more after that in 1940. He was awarded the *Ritterkreuz* on 6 August 1941, the *Eichenlaub* on 9 September 1942 and the *Schwerten* on 23 December 1942. Wilcke was killed in combat with USAAF P-51Bs on 23 March 1944 whilst serving as *Kommodore* of JG 3, having by then been credited with 155 confirmed victories and nine more unconfirmed.

16
Bf 109E-4 <O+I of Oberleutnant Friedrich-Karl Müller, *Stab*. III/JG 53, Le Touquet, October 1940

'Tutti' Müller shot down his first aircraft of the war with 8. *Staffel* on 27 May 1940, and his first of the Battle of Britain (his ninth overall) was not claimed until 5 September. He became the *Gruppen Technischer Offizier* a few days later, only to ditch his Bf 109E-4, Wk-Nr 5251, in the Channel when it ran out of fuel on 15 September. Müller's last victory of 1940 was his tenth, on 6 September. He was killed in a landing accident on 29 May 1944 whilst serving as *Kommodore* of JG 3 (having taken over the *Jagdgeschwader* following the death of fellow 'Pik As' ace 'Furst' Wilcke), by which time he had been awarded the *Ritterkreuz* (19 September 1942) and the *Eichenlaub*, and been credited with 140 victories.

17
Bf 109E-4 <+I of Leutnant Erich Schmidt, *Stab*. III./JG 53, Le Touquet, December 1940

The most successful 'Pik-As' pilot of the Battle of Britain (equal with Hauptmann Heinz Bretnütz of II./JG 53) was Leutnant Erich Schmidt of 9. *Staffel*, whose first victory came on 12 August and last (his 17th) on 30 November. Shortly after this he became *Gruppen* Adjutant before returning to 9. *Staffel*, his place in *Stab*. III./JG 53 being taken by future 49-victory ace Oberleutnant Kurt Quaet-Faslem. Schmidt quickly increased his victory tally to 47 on the Eastern Front, receiving the *Ritterkreuz* on 23 July 1941. He was reported missing in action on 31 August that year, however, his Bf 109F-2 being hit by flak. Although Schmidt was seen to bail out, he remains listed as missing in action.

18
Bf 109E-4 'White 1' of Oberleutnant Heinz Altendorf, *Staffelkapitän* 7./JG 53, Le Touquet, November 1940

Heinz Altendorf's first victory came on 19 May 1940, and by the end of the Battle of France his score had risen to four. He had to wait until 8 September to claim his first success of the Battle of Britain, by which time he was leading 7. *Staffel*. In the process of getting his sixth victory, on 20 September, his Bf 109E-4, Wk-Nr 5175 'White 12', was damaged. Then, on 5 October, Altendorf's Bf 109E-4 Wk-Nr 5372 was written off when he crash-landed at Cap Gris Nez following combat. His seventh victory did not come until 16 May 1941. The aircraft shown here is believed to be the one that replaced the fighter lost on 5 October 1940, as it features six victory bars on its fin. Altendorf had claimed 24 aircraft destroyed by the time he was shot down by flak near Mechili, in Libya, on 16 December 1941 and taken prisoner.

19
Bf 109E-4 'White 6' of Leutnant Herbert Schramm, 7./JG 53, Le Touquet, November 1940

A prewar flying instructor and test pilot for the aircraft manufacturer Siebel, Herbert Schramm began the conflict as an NCO, claiming his first victory on 14 May 1940. This remained unconfirmed, however, and he had to wait 13 more days before he was credited with his first success. He did not claim his next victory until 2 September, and his last of 1940, and as an NCO, was his eighth on 17 October. Schramm was promoted to leutnant the following month and awarded the *Ritterkreuz* on 6 August 1941. He was killed in action fighting USAAF P-47s on 1 December 1943, his victory tally having increased to 40 confirmed and five unconfirmed. Schramm was awarded the *Eichenlaub* posthumously on 11 February 1945.

20
Bf 109E-1 Wk-Nr 5175 'White 12' of Unteroffizier Hermann Neuhoff, 7./JG 53, Rennes, early September 1940

Hermann Neuhoff was reportedly flying this aircraft when he scored his eighth kill, on 11 June 1940, but by the time he shot down his ninth aircraft, on 15 September 1940, he appears to have been in 'White 3'. Minus the kill markings but still coded 'White 12', Wk-Nr 5175 was attacked by Spitfires and crash-landed at Strood, near Rochester, in Kent, on 30 September 1940, Unteroffizier Ernst Poschenreider being taken prisoner. Neuhoff himself was taken prisoner on Malta on 9 April 1942 after being shot down, his tally then standing at 38. He was awarded the *Ritterkreuz* in absentia on 19 June that same year.

21
Bf 109E-4 Wk-Nr 1506 'White 5' of Unteroffizier Hans-Georg Schulte, 7./JG 53, Le Touquet, September 1940

Despite being so junior in rank, Hans-Georg Schulte did well in the Battle of France, shooting down his first aircraft on 14 May and JG 53's last of the campaign, and his third, on 7 June. Schulte's first of the Battle of Britain came on 13 August, but in shooting down his seventh, a Spitfire at 1910 hrs on 6 September, his aircraft was also damaged and he crash-landed at Vincent's Farm near Manston. The RAF noted that the aircraft had a white (as opposed to yellow) spinner, cowling and rudder, and that the red band had been overpainted. It also appears that the fighter had two or maybe three victory bars ahead of the rudder, below the top hinge, and that the swastika had been painted out.

INDEX